In the name of ALLAH (Almighty God),
The Most Beneficent, The Most Merciful

THE IMPRISONMENT OF
IMAM JAMIL ABDULLAH AL-AMIN:
IS IT A GOVERNMENT CONSPIRACY?

EL-HAJJ MAURI SAALAKHAN

(AND OTHER VOICES)

Published in the United States by The Aafia Foundation, Inc. Distributed by The Aafia Foundation, Inc., 11160 Veirs Mill Rd, Ste. LLH18, PMB 298, Silver Spring, MD. 20902

ISBN: 9798 6284 57832

Cover design by Mahrus Abdul-Aliyy

JUSTICE

That justice is a blind goddess

Is a thing to which we blacks are wise

Her bandage hides two festering sores

Which once, perhaps, were eyes.

- Langston Hughes

Acknowledgements

We begin by acknowledging ***The Creator*** of all that exists, The Source of all good. We follow this first and most important acknowledgement with recognition of those who helped make <u>The Imprisonment of Imam Jamil Abdullah Al-Amin: Is It A Government Conspiracy</u> possible.

The late Imam Khalil Abdur-Rahman (may ALLAH be pleased with him) was a constant reminder of the need to update and republish an earlier work on Imam Jamil (as he is commonly known). We salute his memory. The family of Imam Jamil: Sr. Karima Al-Amin, and Brs. Ali and Kairi Al-Amin. (Kairi has gallantly assumed a lead role in the struggle for the freedom of his father.)

We salute Heather Gray of the "Justice Initiative" (producer of WRFG Radio's *"Just Peace"*) and Georgia State University Professor Akinyele Umoja for helping to insure that Imam Jamil Abdullah Al-Amin (the former H. Rap Brown) would not be forgotten on the home front. Heather gave us permission to include the thought-provoking interview she did with Dr. Harry Edwards on the 1968 Olympics Protest (and for this we are grateful). We also thank contributors Obaid H. Siddiqui, Hamzah Raza, Masood Abdul Haqq, Imam Khalid Griggs, and Dr. Cornel West.

A special note of thanks must also be extended to Ambassador Andrew Young, for having the courage and conscience to publicly raise his concerns regarding Imam Jamil's ongoing imprisonment.

Last, but certainly not least, we acknowledge the advocacy work of the Imam Jamil Action Network (IJAN); and supporters of The Aafia Foundation throughout the US who have made our human rights work possible. May ALLAH's blessings be upon you all.

Introduction

March 16, 2020, marks 20 years since the tragedy unfolded in Atlanta, Georgia, that would have a traumatic impact on *many* lives. Today Imam Jamil Abdullah Al-Amin (the former H. Rap Brown) is Prisoner # 99974-555 in a federal institution in Tucson, Arizona.

It should be noted that for most of these years, Imam Jamil (as he is commonly known), *a state prisoner*, was housed in the federal government's only "supermax" prison located in Florence, Colorado. While he no longer resides in that facility, he still remains under special administrative measures – imprisonment conditions which continue to take a toll on his health.

"The Case of Imam Jamil Abdullah Al-Amin: Is It A Government Conspiracy?" was first published in 2002, as a small booklet in the aftermath of what masqueraded as a "fair trial" in downtown Atlanta. Our intent in publishing the booklet was to brief concerned folk around the nation on the substance of his case. The booklet has been out-of-print for a number of years, but the struggle for justice continues. Those of us who believe in Imam Jamil's innocence felt the need to reissue the publication with more *exculpatory* evidence for the court of public opinion to consider.

"The Imprisonment of Imam Jamil Abdullah Al-Amin: Is It A Government Conspiracy" is now a small book with other voices brought into the mix beyond my own. Through this updated treatise, we pray that many of the readers unfamiliar with the life and legacy of Imam Jamil will gain a deeper appreciation for who he is; a deeper sensitivity for where he is; and a deeper awareness of how he came to be where he is. After that, let your own conscience be your guide.

In the struggle for peace thru justice,

El-Hajj Mauri' Saalakhan

Table of Contents

Prologue: From H. Rap to Al-Amin

The Following Prologue, with a few minor modifications, is republished here courtesy of Writers' Inc., publishers of Revolution By The Book; a thought-provoking treatise on the fundamental tenets of Islam, authored by Imam Jamil Abdullah Al-Amin (the former H. Rap Brown).

In the late 1960's, he was known as H. Rap Brown, Chairman of the Student Nonviolent Coordinating Committee, (SNCC); Minister of Justice of the Black Panther Party; and as someone who made the FBI's most-wanted list.[1] He later became known as Jamil Abdullah Al-Amin, *Imam* (spiritual leader) of an international Muslim community based in Atlanta, Georgia.

As a Muslim leader, Imam Al-Amin is recognized for his dedication to the principles of the Holy Qur'an and the tradition of Prophet Muhammad (may the peace and blessings of ALLAH be upon him). He frequently spoke at universities and Islamic organization conferences and conventions. More than 17 communities throughout North America and the Caribbean pledged allegiance to his leadership.

After a life-time of involvement in the struggle of African-American people for justice and liberation, the commitment of Imam Al-Amin never wavered. He stated:

> The struggle is an ongoing process. Many times, people mistakenly identify movement as struggle. Movement is only a phase of struggle. When the first slave rebelled against being a slave, he gave an alternative to slavery that has been built upon until now. That's struggle, and there have been many movements in the struggle -- the *abolitionist* movement, the

---

[1] On the 25th anniversary of the riot which rocked Cambridge, Maryland in 1967, *City Paper* staff writer John Lewis interviewed Imam Al-Amin and wrote an in-depth article on the disturbance. We are grateful for the permission granted by *City Paper* for use of material from that article in this prologue. *City Paper* (Baltimore, Maryland), Vol. 16, No. 4, January 24, 1992. -----?

antislavery movement, the *civil rights* movement, the *free speech* movement.

It means they come, they serve a purpose, and they go out. We grew to understand that it was a vehicle that moved people from one level of understanding to another level. The civil rights movement had to go out. It's ridiculous [today] to try to re-live it; but the struggle still goes on.

The mission of a believer in Islam is totally different from coexisting or being a part of the system. The prevailing morals are wrong. Their ethics are wrong. Western philosophy has reduced man to food, clothing, shelter, and the sex drive, which means he doesn't have a spirit. In Islam, we're not talking about getting the poor to vote. We're not talking about empowering poor people with money. We're talking about overturning that whole thing, man. (*City Paper*, January 12, 1992)

Brown, the youngest of three children, was born in Baton Rouge, Louisiana, in 1943. His father worked as a laborer for Esso Standard Oil; his mother taught children at an orphanage and also worked as a maid.

As a youth, the 6'5" Brown was an excellent athlete, excelling in basketball and football. After graduating from high school, he attended Southern University, in Baton Rouge, but did not find the school a place with which he could identify. It was apparent to Brown that an insidious reality existed all around him but went unmentioned.

"It was from watching white people, what they had, and what we had, that I learned about this country," Brown wrote in his part-autobiography, part-political handbook, *Die Nigger Die!* (published in 1969 by Dial Press). "I lived near Louisiana State University, and I could see this big fine school with modern buildings, and it was for whites. Then there was Southern University, which was about to fall in and that was for the [blacks]. And when I compared the two, the message that the white man was trying to get across was obvious...*Die Nigger Die.*"

Brown states that he "knew who I wanted to identify with. It was the bloods in my neighborhood, the guys who hung out down on the corner...I always hung out with cats who had made hanging out a profession. I found that it took special skills to hang out for 14 hours, just laying and playing."

The name given to him by his parents was Hubert Giroir Brown. The street named him Rap. He had a scathing dexterity with the language, combining profound intellect with blunt coarseness. "We played the Dozens like white folks play Scrabble...a mean game, where you try to totally destroy somebody else with words."

Influenced by his readings of many writers committed to the struggle of Blacks for freedom, the nineteen-year-old H. Rap Brown found the environment around Howard University in Washington, D.C. inspiring and motivating. He had spent summers there with his brother (the late Ed Brown) who attended Howard, and by 1964, Brown had moved there and become politically involved in SNCC, the Student Nonviolent Coordinating Committee.

SNCC, in the early 1960's, had initiated peaceful protests and demonstrations to accelerate desegregation in the South. In 1964, SNCC promoted the Mississippi Project, in which about 800 volunteers helped thousands of Blacks register to vote. Under the leadership of Stokely Carmichael, SNCC, in 1966, rejected its earlier policy of nonviolence. It adopted a strong anti-white direction, dissuading whites from participating in the organization and disdaining their support. As chairman of SNCC, Carmichael criticized many of the tactics of the civil rights movement and demanded "Black Power" for his people.

Brown's boldness and commitment were soon recognized by the SNCC leadership. He was sent by Carmichael into Alabama to organize the state. Wrote Brown of those efforts, "At first, we just spent our time going to meetings and getting to know the people. Up in Greene County, we used to starve like dogs. The house we lived in didn't have running water and it had newspapers on the walls and the floors."

H. Rap Brown's reputation and influence grew rapidly. He took on the political establishment with fearless verbal assaults that moved and inspired audiences. He helped break the spell which years of slavery and segregation had cast over the African-American masses who held white leaders in awe and reverence.

In May 1967, at the age of 23, he was elected chairman of SNCC, succeeding Carmichael. *Newsweek* magazine described the new chairman as, "A disenchanted ex-poverty worker who affects sunglasses indoors and out, a droopy mustache, a bushy "natural" coif and a curdled view of the white world... He preaches armed eye-for-an-eye self-defense for Negroes and packs a 12-gauge 'cracker gun' in his own dusty Plymouth."

A national figure, H. Rap Brown was in great demand as a speaker. In July 1967, he addressed a civil rights rally in Cambridge, Maryland, an Eastern shore town of approximately 13,000 people. Brown arrived late and a crowd had already gathered in the streets of the city's Black neighborhood, along with a contingent of police and National Guardsmen.

Reportedly, Brown addressed the crowd in his usual fiery style. From the hood of a parked car, he stormed: "Take your violence to the honkies...You've got to get some guns...Burn and tear Cambridge down! If Cambridge doesn't come around, burn it down...Get yourselves some guns. This town is ready to explode...If you don't have guns, don't be here. You have to be prepared to die..."[*City Paper*, p. 12.]

"After I spoke, people were just milling around. A young lady who lived up towards Race Street, where a bunch of white policemen were, asked me to walk her home, because she was afraid to go by herself. Myself and two other people were walking her home, and some dudes opened fire on us with shotguns from the bushes. We found out later [the gunmen] were black policemen. I was hit. They were shooting at us a long time, and after I got hit, I dove to the ground, rolled over, and made my way over to a ditch and went into somebody's yard.

"After the shooting, there was a lot of commotion, man. People went out in the street and just started tearing everything up, and a few hours later, they burned the school again. Two weeks before I came over and spoke, people had burned the Black elementary school, because it had been a rat-infested, roach-infested place. People were paying their tax dollars, and the students were forced to go to a school in that condition. It was terrible, man... conditions cause riots, not rhetoric." [*City Paper*, p. 12.]

The aftermath: Pine Street Elementary School, along with two blocks of homes and businesses, went up in flames. Brown disappeared, some say concealed in a coffin and driven out of Cambridge in a hearse. Maryland State Police and the FBI issued warrants for his arrest. Two days later, he was arrested by FBI agents in Washington, D.C.'s National Airport and charged with unlawful flight to avoid prosecution. Three weeks later, the State of Maryland charged Brown with inciting to riot.

Freed on $100,000 bond, Brown continued to speak boldly to the nation. In 1967, within hearing distance of the White House in Washington, D.C., he roared, "If you're going to loot, loot yourself a gun store. You got to arm yourself, brother." In Detroit, he declared: *"Violence is as American as cherry pie* [a quote enshrined in Bartlett's Familiar Quotations]. This country has delivered an ultimatum to Black people. America says to Blacks, you either fight to live or you will live to die. I say to America, Freedom or death." [*City Paper*, p. 12.]

By 1968, much of SNCC's leadership had merged into the Black Panther Party, which had been organized in Oakland, California, by Huey P. Newton and Bobby Seale. The Black Panthers called for neighborhood control of such services as education and the police. More importantly, they supported the use of guns for self-defense and to protect the oppressed. The FBI labelled them, "The most dangerous and violence prone of all extremist groups." Brown became the Panther's Minister of Justice.

In December 1969, a police raid on Panther quarters in Chicago resulted in the deaths of two Panther leaders. Police riddled the apartment with bullets in a controversial show of force. Earlier the same year, Seale and other Panthers had been charged with killing a suspected informer. An undeclared war was being waged against the Panthers. Brown's attorney, William Kunstler, who also defended the Chicago 7 and other Black Panthers, delayed Brown's trial for two years. Scheduled to appear on March 10, 1970 for trial, Brown did not appear. That night, two of his associates, Ralph Featherstone and William Payne, were killed when a bomb exploded in their car. At the rescheduled date of his trial, May 4, 1970, Brown again failed to appear. Two days later, the FBI listed Brown as one of its most wanted fugitives.

Brown eluded the FBI for a year and a half. On October 16, 1971, he surfaced. With three supporters who had joined him he led an attack on a New York City bar, targeted for its exploitation of the community [word on the street labeled it a 'drug den']. A shootout with police ensued and Brown was wounded, captured, and taken to the detention facilities at Rikers Island. Behind bars, awaiting his trial, he recalls that "the Muslims would come inside the prison and they would have services on Friday. They extended an invitation for me to come down to services and I attended. I came down to *Jumu'ah,* but I didn't become Muslim at first.

[In the struggle] we were familiar with Islam in different ways, because there was a lot of conversation in the media...of Malcolm X, his odyssey from early life to being a Muslim when he died; he was a visible image and I'm sure his conversion to true Islam had an impact on many different people. It made me look at Islam even more seriously than I would have ...I began to ask myself, "in terms of what they are talking about, what's wrong with it?" I couldn't find anything wrong. It caused me to investigate it even more, which required my becoming a Muslim. [*City Paper*, p. 11.]

According to Brother Jamil, becoming a Muslim was no more than "a continuation of a lifestyle. See, most people don't have a true picture of what Islam is. Islam is not nonviolent. There is a right to self-defense, and there is a right to defend your faith. Allah says that fighting is prescribed for you. Fight tyranny and oppression, for tyranny and oppression are worse than slaughter, so fight them wherever you may find them."

It became evident that to accomplish the things we had talked about in the struggle, you would need a practice. Allah says He does not change the condition of people until they change that which is in themselves. That is what Islam does, and it points out right from wrong. It points out truth from falsehood... [*City Paper*, p. 11.]

H. Rap Brown made his declaration of faith in late 1971. Henceforth, his name would be Jamil Abdullah Al-Amin. He was to remain imprisoned at Rikers Island until 1972, when he was moved to a jail in Long Island City and then to the Tombs. His trial for armed robbery and assaulting a police officer was finally brought to court in 1973:

It was a strange fare for a jury to digest, beginning as it did with a prayer and ending enigmatically with a poem. Before a hushed courtroom crowd, [H. Rap Brown]...took his lawyer's place to deliver the opening statement...in blue jeans and beige knit skullcap, he stood quietly with his head bowed for several moments, palms extended heavenward, murmuring a Muslim prayer. [*Newsweek*, February 12, 1973.]

He was sentenced to five-to-fifteen years in Attica State Prison, but after three years in various state prisons, Brother Jamil won parole in 1976. His total jail and prison time was five years, including two years in jail prior to sentencing.

He resettled in Atlanta and soon organized a small community of Muslims. With pooled resources of the brothers and sisters, a small house was purchased on West End Place to serve as the *masjid*. Brother Jamil was selected as *Imam*. He had studied intensely, learned Qur'an and *Sunnah*, and, of course, his leadership qualities were still intact. The Atlanta community would grow to number around 400

members; with businesses and two purchased lots adjacent to the
masjid – with the intent to house a larger masjid, a community center,
and an Islamic school.

Imam Al-Amin stresses, however, that "any building is just an
edifice. The mosque is built to make prayer. Prayer is the key to the
community, not buildings. The Islamic program is built around the
making of prayer, and we've been able to establish and maintain the
prayer."

Allah has allowed me to understand that it is not race or color that
is the issue. The only important thing is the word of ALLAH. Since
Islam, I understand that truth is not relative. Truth is universal. There
is no god but ALLAH. It is the truth on which the whole universe
rests, and nothing changes that. [*City Paper*, p. 15].

CHAPTER 1 - A Chronological Sketch

The information in this opening chapter is very important for helping the reader to understand the seamless connections between H. Rap Brown and Imam Jamil Abdullah Al-Amin. Most importantly, the undeniable fact that this militant activist turned spiritual leader remained a target for neutralization throughout his public life.

Imam Jamil's Cases and Activities over the Years

"There are two ways of fighting; one with arms, and the other with law."
– Nicolo Machiavelli, The Prince

Imam Jamil Abdullah Al-Amin, formerly known as H. Rap Brown, was born in Baton Rouge, Louisiana, on October 4, 1943. He attended primary and high school in the city of his birth. The following is a sketch of Imam Jamil's civil and human rights history. In reviewing the outline provided by the wife of Imam Jamil, Sr. Karima Al-Amin, Esq., I was reminded of that highly informative **"Re-Learning H. Rap Brown National Conference,"** spearheaded by Professor Akinyele Umoja, in October of 2019.

The array of speakers from around the US who converged in Atlanta (GA) for that well-organized two-day "Teach-in," were excellent! Please pay special attention, in the outline that follows, to how "law" was used as a weapon of war against H. Rap Brown (and other activists) during his generation's sojourn into the *African American human rights struggle.*

The 1960s

1960-1964

H. Rap Brown attended Southern University in Baton Rouge, Louisiana. After completing three years at Southern University, he left Louisiana to work with the Nonviolent Action Group (NAG). During the summers of 1962 and 63, he worked with NAG in Washington, D.C. In 1964, he was elected chairperson and worked to bring the college students and African American community together.

He spent much of the summer of 1964 with the Mississippi Summer Project and the Mississippi Freedom Democratic Party (MFDP). He attended the Atlantic City Democratic Convention as part of the MFDP.

1964-1965

H. Rap Brown was employed by the Department of Agriculture during the year, and also worked as a neighborhood worker for an anti-poverty program in Washington, D.C.

1966-1967

H. Rap Brown was appointed Director of the Greene County Project in Alabama for the Student Nonviolent Coordinating Committee (SNCC) and was responsible for organizing projects in the state of Alabama. Law enforcement agencies immediately monitored his activities and leveled several infractions against him, *especially during times of county and state elections.* As an organizer, Brown was instrumental in organizing the Black vote.

In May 1967, H. Rap Brown was elected Chairman of SNCC, succeeding Stokely Carmichael (later to become known as Kwame Ture).

July 24, 1967

H. Rap Brown was invited by a local civil rights group and Gloria Richardson to address a rally in Cambridge, Maryland. Immediately following the speech, while walking with a group down Race Street, he received a gunshot wound to his forehead as local police officers fired shots into the group of Black community residents. About four hours after Brown left the state, the Pine Street Elementary School burned. This school had burned twice before and was a shell at the time of the July 24th burning.

He was treated for his gunshot wound immediately after being shot, and prepared for a drive to Washington, D.C. The police followed his auto to the Maryland state line and watched him leave the state. A fugitive warrant was then issued, which shortly thereafter became a federal warrant—*a descendant of the Fugitive Slave Act.*

The U. S. Attorney issued the federal warrant, and H. Rap Brown was charged with counseling to arson and inciting to arson and riot.

July 25, 1967

The FBI made arrangements with Attorney William Kunstler to have his client, H. Rap Brown, surrender to the FBI in lower Manhattan (New York City) at 11:00 AM, on July 26, 1967.

July 26, 1967

The FBI arrested H. Rap Brown at the National Airport in Virginia while he was enroute to New York to surrender at the prearranged time and place. He was taken to Alexandria, Virginia, released by the federal authorities, then re-arrested by Alexandria, Virginia police officials. Brown was later released on $10,000 bail.

August 1, 1967

While on a trip to Dayton, Ohio, to make a speech, officials charged
H. Rap Brown with "advocating criminal syndicalism." No
indictment was pressed.

August 14, 1967

H. Rap Brown traveled to Baton Rouge, Louisiana, from New York
City to visit his parents. During his travel he carried a rifle and
checked it with airline authorities. On this same day, unbeknownst to
him, Brown was indicted in Maryland on the arson and riot charges.

August 18, 1967

H. Rap Brown returned to New York City.

August 19, 1967

H. Rap Brown was arrested at 2:00 AM in New York City and charged with two violations of the Federal Firearms Act, which makes it "unlawful for any person who is under indictment for a crime punishable by imprisonment for a term exceeding one year: to ship, transport, in interstate or foreign commerce, any firearm or ammunition." The new charge was based on the August 14th indictment. (The Maryland arson charge carried an imprisonment term of more than one year.)

H. Rap Brown was taken back to Louisiana, and bail was set at $25,000. It was later reduced to $15,000 and he was released with a bond restriction confining him to the Southern District of New York—Manhattan, Bronx, and nine counties within the Westchester jurisdiction. The District Court stipulated that Brown could only travel when permitted by the Court at its discretion.

January 11, 1968

H. Rap Brown was charged with intimidating/assaulting a New York City police officer as he and another SNCC worker were leaving the lobby of the Cuban Mission. The incident occurred after the officer inquired about a package the SNCC worker was carrying. Brown remained in the Embassy for hours and was released after his attorneys held legal discussions with the NYPD. This charge was dropped in February 1968.

February 18-20, 1968

H. Rap Brown traveled to California to confer with his attorneys. While in California he was invited to speak at a Black Panther rally and did so with his attorneys present.

February 20, 1968

H. Rap Brown returned to New York City and was arrested approximately seven hours later. He was charged with violating the terms of his previous bond, which restricted him to the Southern District of New York. Brown's legal counsel maintained that trips to confer with attorneys were allowed by the Court. He was released in New York and required to appear in New Orleans the following day.

February 21, 1968

Judge Lansing Mitchell set a $50,000 bail in New Orleans. During the court recess, H. Rap Brown was charged with threatening an FBI agent in the court hallway. Witnesses took the stand on Brown's behalf describing the incident. However, the judge, a former FBI agent, set a $50,000 bail on that charge and Brown was jailed on a total of $100,000 bail.

April 11, 1968

While H. Rap Brown was in New Orleans Parish Prison, the *"Rap Brown" Federal Anti-Riot Act* was passed. The legislation passed several days after the assassination of Dr. Martin Luther King, Jr., and was tagged onto a fair housing bill at the last minute by the late Strom Thurmond. The "Rap Brown" amendment was later used by the government to prosecute "dissenters" - including the Chicago 8, Wounded Knee defendants, and anti-war activists.

April 19, 1968

H. Rap Brown remained in Parish Prison, fasting a total of 48 days, until April 19th, when bail finally was reduced by the Fifth Circuit Court of Appeals from $100,000 to a total of $30,000; $15,000 on the travel violation, and $15,000 on the intimidation charge. Bond was posted and Brown was taken directly to Virginia where the judge refused to set bail. Brown waived extradition and was taken immediately to Maryland and released on bond.

May 13-22, 1968

Over objections from H. Rap Brown's attorneys, trial on the federal firearms charge was held less than a month from his release in New Orleans. The jury found Brown innocent of carrying the rifle to New Orleans while under indictment, but guilty of carrying the rifle back to New York while under indictment. The government presented news clippings, along with television and radio personnel as witnesses, who stated, stories concerning the Maryland indictment were broadcast from August 16-18, 1967; therefore, Brown should have known he was under indictment. Judge Mitchell sentenced him to the maximum sentence of five years and a $2,000 fine. Brown was continued on the original $15,000 bond, pending appeal. He returned to New York City and continued his confinement to the Southern and Eastern Districts of New York.

August 29, 1968

The New York Times reported that the Republican Party leader of the House, Gerald Ford of Michigan, stated it was time to "slam the door" on H. Rap Brown and other Black power advocates. Gerald Ford and Everett McKinley Dirksen of Illinois cited Republican backing of the House-passed anti-riot bill. Ford maintained that the anti-riot bill could be used against H. Rap Brown, while Dirksen felt there were existing laws on the books that could be used against him.

April 3, 1969

H. Rap Brown's five-year sentence on the technical firearms charge was vacated by the U.S. Court of Appeals for the 5th Circuit, and the matter was remanded to the District Court for an electronic surveillance hearing.

1970s-1980s

March 9, 1970

Almost three years after the Cambridge, Maryland incident, the state of Maryland selected Bel Air, Maryland, as the site for H. Rap Brown's trial on counseling and inciting to arson and riot. Pre-trial hearings were scheduled over the objections of Brown's attorneys.

During the morning hours, a vehicle carrying two SNCC organizers, Ralph Featherstone and William Che Payne, exploded; both men were killed.

March 10, 1970

H. Rap Brown failed to appear for a hearing in Bel Air, Maryland.

April 20, 1970

The trial site was changed to Ellicott City, Maryland. Brown did not appear for trial.

May 6, 1970

Based on the federal charge of violating the Federal Firearms Act, the Maryland charge of inciting to arson and riot, and the federal charge of intimidating an FBI agent, the FBI placed H. Rap Brown on the "10 Most Wanted List."

A hearing on a wiretap issue was held in New Orleans, Louisiana. The Court ruled that all wiretap material was irrelevant to the Federal Firearms indictment, conviction, and sentence.

September 24, 1970

Judge Lansing Mitchell imposed the maximum sentence of five years, $2,000 fine in H. Rap Brown's absence.

January 11, 1971

Reporter Robert Woodward revealed that Dorchester County state's attorney, William B. Yates, stated to the Howard County state's attorney, Richard J. Kinlein, that the arson charge against H. Rap Brown was fabricated to insure involvement of the FBI. This arson charge, a felony, was also essential to the Federal Firearms arrest, indictment, and conviction.

October 16, 1971

H. Rap Brown was shot and beaten on a rooftop on the west side of New York City by police officers. He subsequently was charged with 24 counts of robbery, attempted murder, and possession of weapons, and was held under a $250,000 bail.

October 19, 1971

The Maryland State Attorney Kinlein, who revealed to Robert Woodward that he was told the Maryland charge against Brown was fabricated, was convicted of contempt of court and fined $350.00 for making a statement "prejudicial to a fair trial." However, no action was taken against the prosecutor who admitted the fabrication to Kinlein. The prosecutor, William Yates, would later deny the allegation.

December 1971

H. Rap Brown takes his shahada in the Rikers Island (New York) jail and proclaims he is a Muslim with the name Jamil Abdullah Al-Amin.

March 17, 1972

Jamil Abdullah Al-Amin moved to reinstate his appeal on the federal firearms conviction. The Fifth Circuit Court of Appeals set aside the sentence based on the fact that Judge Mitchell sentenced him in absentia—an improper act.

June 2, 1972

Although Al-Amin was recovering from wounds sustained in October 1971, Judge Mitchell obtained a writ to have him moved for resentencing to New Orleans from New York City, where he was awaiting trial. Al-Amin's attorneys argued for Judge Mitchell to reduce the sentence. At the time of sentencing and in 1968, Al-Amin did not have a record of prior convictions. Mitchell, however, imposed the maximum sentence of five years and a $2,000 fine, and stipulated that this sentence not begin until New York released him. This was ordered even though Al-Amin was awaiting trial in New York and was electing not to post the $200,000 bail, reduced from $250,000 in February 1972.

October 23, 1972

One week before the scheduled start of the New York trial, *New York Magazine* published an article written by a former Commissioner of the New York City Police Department. The article was an attempt to describe dramatically the events of the morning of October 16, 1971, as told by police officers. It was highly prejudicial to Jamil Abdullah Al-Amin and extremely inaccurate. The attorney representing the magazine and writer conceded that various sections of the article contained misrepresentations. The District Attorney maintained he had not encouraged the printing of the story, and the trial judge refuses the defense motion for dismissal. As a result, Al-Amin filed a damage suit against the magazine, the writer, and New York City Police Department.

January 15, 1973

After preliminary trial hearings in November and December, and after three weeks of jury selection, Al-Amin and three codefendants began trial in New York.

March 29, 1973

The jury returned a guilty verdict on six counts of robbery, three counts of assault in the first degree, and two counts of possession of a weapon. The jury remained deadlocked on the three counts of attempted murder and was dismissed from any further deliberation.

April 1973

The government was ordered to prosecute or dismiss, and the government chose to dismiss the 1968 indictment charging Al-Amin with intimidating a FBI agent. Judge Mitchell recused himself from hearing the case based on the fact he was a former FBI agent and might therefore be partial (toward the prosecution). He refused, however, to recuse himself from any hearings on the 1968 federal firearms conviction.

May 9, 1973

H. Rap Brown/Jamil Abdullah Al-Amin was sentenced in New York to concurrent terms of 0-15 years on each robbery count, five to 15 years on the assault count, and 0 to 7 years on each weapon count.

September 1973

The Fifth Circuit Court of Appeals refused to overturn the New Orleans conviction.

October 1973

Al-Amin filed a brief before the Supreme Court based on the wiretap
issue in the New Orleans case. The Supreme Court subsequently
declined to review the case. Justice William O. Douglass dissented.

November 2, 1973

Al-Amin was transported from Attica Correctional Facility to
Baltimore, Maryland, to stand trial on the 1967 charge of inciting to
riot and arson.

November 6, 1973

The Maryland Prosecutor, who admitted the fabrication of the arson
charge to Kinlein, announced during preliminary hearings that the
state would not prosecute. Al-Amin was arraigned on a misdemeanor
charge of failing to appear after forfeiture of bond. He received the
maximum one-year imprisonment sentence and a $1,000 fine to run
concurrently, as of October 16, 1971, with the New York sentence.

April 29, 1974

A New Orleans patent attorney wrote William Kunstler stating that
prior to the 1968 trial in New Orleans he overheard the trial judge,
Lansing Mitchell, state to a group of friends at a Louisiana Bar
Convention in Biloxi, Mississippi, that since he was just told he would
preside over the "Rap Brown" trial, he wanted to take care of his
health so that he could *"get that nigger."* Al-Amin's attorneys
immediately filed timely motions challenging the conviction and
sentence.

January 24, 1975

Jamil Abdullah Al-Amin was transported to New Orleans for a hearing
on overturning the 1968 conviction, or reducing the five-year

maximum sentence, based on Mitchell's prejudicial pretrial statement and recently revealed governmental misconduct (COINTELPRO).

Another judge heard the argument, believed the patent attorney, and noted that Judge Mitchell probably made the statement. Months later, however, the judge refused to overturn the conviction or reduce the sentence. *The government was forced, at the January 24th hearing, to admit Al-Amin was mentioned as a "target" in sections of the COINTELPRO document.September 1975*

Al-Amin's attorneys filed an appeal in New York challenging the New York conviction.

December 17, 1975

Al-Amin's attorneys filed an appeal on the New Orleans conviction before the Fifth Circuit Court of Appeals. The appeal raised the validity of the 1968 conviction and sentence, based on Mitchell's "get that nigger" statement and the government's admitted COINTELPRO misconduct. *Additional surveillance memos from the U.S. Navy Department were obtained through the Freedom of Information Act and incorporated into the appeal.*

May 13, 1976

Al-Amin's attorneys, William M. Kunstler and Elizabeth Schneider, engaged in oral argument before the Fifth Circuit Court of Appeals challenging the 1968 New Orleans conviction and sentence.

May 28, 1976

The State of New York answered Al-Amin's New York appeal; an oral argument before the Appellate Division was scheduled for June 1976.

June 1976

The Appellate Division refused to overturn Al-Amin's 1973 New York conviction.

October 11, 1976

Jamil Abdullah Al-Amin appeared before the New York State Parole Board. He served the five-year minimum sentence ordered by the New York trial judge. Hundreds of letters were sent to the parole board in support of his release. Al-Amin was released. In addition, the federal government dropped the Louisiana charges and New York permitted the Imam to transfer his parole to Atlanta, Georgia.

November 1976

Newly released Jamil Abdullah Al-Amin travels to Saudi Arabia for his *hajj* and returns to Atlanta, Georgia to organize a Muslim community in the southwest part of the city (West End).

October 1986

Imam Jamil completes his parole supervision in Atlanta, Georgia, and was released from parole.

1990s-2000s

A new phase of surveillance and harassment begins.

August 7, 1995

Imam Jamil was arrested in Atlanta by the ATF, FBI, and a police officer on loan to the FBI's counter-terrorism task force, on suspicion of aggravated assault on a neighborhood resident. He was charged with aggravated assault and carrying a concealed weapon without a permit. The alleged victim never identified the imam as the suspect, although city and government agents attempted to pressure him into doing so.

August 8, 1995

Imam Jamil was released from jail on a $27,500 bail. The City of Atlanta and the federal government failed to indict the imam on the alleged charges. The victim embraced Islam and joined the community as a worshipper at Imam Jamil's masjid in the West End of Atlanta, Georgia.

May 31, 1999

Imam Jamil was stopped by a Cobb County police officer while driving in Marietta (part of Cobb County, Georgia). He was cited and arrested for driving a vehicle that *allegedly* was reported stolen and having no proof of insurance. The police officer searched Imam Jamil's wallet and saw a badge; without questioning him further, the officer added the charge of "impersonating a police officer."

Imam Jamil was released on a $10,000 bond; and subsequently presented evidence from the mayor of Whitehall, Alabama, to the Cobb County prosecutor's office, which confirmed his appointment as an auxiliary officer for youth in the town of Whitehall, Alabama. In addition, affidavits were submitted that countered the "theft by receiving" a stolen vehicle charge.

January 28, 2000

Imam Jamil's Cobb County case was scheduled for a trial call. A storm caused the Superior Court of Cobb County to experience delays in the calendar calls. Imam Jamil did not have legal representation that day, and the Imam received no further notification concerning the case.

March 16, 2000

Shortly before 10:00 PM, two deputies of the Fulton County Sheriff's Department approached Imam Jamil's store, in the West End of

Atlanta, to serve a bench warrant for the imam's failure to appear in Cobb County for trial - stemming from the May 31, 1999, arrest. The store was closed, and they left. The deputies returned and upon seeing an individual in the street outside the store a confrontation ensued and shots were fired.

One deputy was killed and the other remained in the hospital, suffering from gunshot wounds. Although conflicting identification details were given of the assailant, none matching Imam Jamil (*and the assailant was reportedly shot*), the surviving deputy purportedly identified the imam. As a result, various state, local, and federal agencies launched a massive manhunt for "Jamil Al-Amin / aka, H. Rap Brown."

March 20, 2000

Imam Jamil was arrested in White Hall, Alabama, and subsequently charged with the murder of one deputy and the wounding of another. After he was taken into custody, a handcuffed Imam Jamil (laying prone on the ground) is kicked and spat upon by an out of control FBI agent with a history of misconduct. Imam Jamil is taken to Montgomery, Alabama, where he stayed for one month fighting extradition to Georgia. While in the Montgomery Detention Center, Imam Jamil was indicted in Georgia on 13 counts – which included felony murder, aggravated assault upon a peace officer, obstruction of a law enforcement officer, possession of a firearm by a convicted felon, and possession of a firearm during commission of a felony.

During his Montgomery (AL) detention he was represented by Alabama attorneys J. L. Chestnut, Rose Sanders, and Georgia attorney, Musa Dan-Fodio.

April 21, 2000

Imam Jamil was moved from Montgomery, Alabama, to Cobb County, Georgia, and placed in the Cobb County Adult Detention Center.

April 24, 2000

Imam Jamil appeared before a Cobb County Magistrate who explained the Cobb County charges.

May 4, 2000

Imam Jamil made his first appearance in Fulton County Superior Court. Two Georgia attorneys, Jack Martin and Bruce Harvey, were approved and appointed by the Superior Court of Fulton County to represent the Imam on the Fulton County charges. The Fulton County DA announced that it would seek the death penalty, and the attorneys for Imam Jamil filed numerous motions.

May 31, 2000

Imam Jamil appeared in Fulton County Superior Court. Among the issues addressed was the violation by Sheriff Jackie Barrett of a restrictive order; she released transmission tapes of one of the deputies calling for help while shots were being fired on the evening of March

16, 2000. The Superior Court judge found Sheriff Barrett in "constructive contempt" of the restrictive order.

June 22, 2000

Imam Jamil is transferred to the Fulton County Jail from the Cobb County Adult Detention Center.

June 28, 2000

Imam Jamil appeared in Fulton County Superior Court where Judge Stephanie Manis announced she had been randomly selected to be the presiding trial judge. Issues were discussed relative to the discovery process and a timetable for the district attorney to produce scientific findings and photographs.

January-March 9, 2002

Jury selection begins in the Superior Court of Fulton County, Georgia, with Imam Jamil's team of four attorneys—Jack Martin, Bruce Harvey, Tony Axam, and Michael Warren of New York. The trial ultimately lasts for just three weeks, with the jury taking less than 10 hours to reach a guilty verdict on all 13 counts.

March 11, 2002

The sentencing phase begins. Imam Jamil's defense team called twenty character witnesses. The witnesses included civil rights icon - former US ambassador, and former mayor for the city of Atlanta - Andrew Young, along with an array of civic, academic and religious leaders, and human rights activists. Each testified on the imam's behalf in an effort to prevent imposition of the death penalty.

March 14, 2002

The jury announced a sentence of **life without the possibility of parole** on the two counts of murder and felony murder; the judge imposed an additional 30 years to the sentence as punishment on the remaining 11 counts. Imam Jamil is moved immediately to Jackson, Georgia, and then on to the Reidsville Maximum Security State Prison, in southern Georgia.

May 24, 2004

Georgia Supreme Court affirmed Imam Jamil's convictions.

June 28, 2004

The Georgia Supreme Court denies Imam Jamil's Motion for Reconsideration.

November 2004

In response to grievances filed by Imam Jamil, the Georgia Department of Corrections ruled that Reidsville violated standard operating procedures by opening mail clearly marked "legal" from Imam Jamil's wife (Karima Al-Amin) who is an attorney.

November 14, 2005

Counsel for Imam Jamil filed a habeas corpus (*Jamil Abdullah Al-Amin* v. *Hugh Smith*) in the Superior Court of Tattnall County, Georgia. The habeas corpus cited 14 grounds for reversal of Imam Jamil's conviction and sentence, including the failure of his trial and appellate attorneys to investigate the individual who confessed to the charges shortly after the March 2000 incident.

February 27, 2007

A habeas hearing is held in Tattnall County where Imam Jamil is able to testify. Imam Jamil is able to highlight the ineffective assistance of counsel.

August 2, 2007

The public learns that Imam Jamil (a <u>state</u> prisoner) has been moved, without notice to his attorneys or family members, to Oklahoma City; and from there to the Supermax federal prison in Florence, Colorado.

August 15, 2007

Imam Jamil is finally able to communicate with his attorneys that he was moved from Reidsville to an airport where he became ill. He was taken to the Atlanta Medical Center for two days of exploratory tests for chest pains, and then placed in federal custody. This move to a federal prison without a federal charge, conviction, or sentence, was made possible based on a March 1990 Agreement between the Georgia Department of Corrections and the Federal Bureau of Prisons to accept a state prisoner for monthly compensation.

Prior to this move, Georgia Muslim inmates initiated an effort to name Imam Jamil as "the imam for all Muslim inmates" in the Georgia prison system. The Department of Corrections requested that Imam Jamil ask the inmates to discontinue this effort. However, the FBI initiated an investigation in 2007, labeling its report, *"The Radicalization of Muslim Inmates in the Georgia Prison System."* It becomes clear that Imam Jamil's transfer into federal custody is a direct outgrowth of the FBI's involvement.

September 20, 2007

Attorneys from Kilpatrick Stockton argue before the 11th Circuit Court of Appeals on behalf of Imam Jamil, citing a First Amendment violation when the staff at Reidsville opened his legal mail.

January 7, 2008

The 11th Circuit Court of Appeals ruled the Reidsville warden and staff violated Imam Jamil's First Amendment rights by opening legal mail from his wife outside of his presence, which ultimately results in a settlement for the violation.

July 28, 2011

After six years, Judge Rose of Tattnall County, Georgia, denied Imam Jamil's habeas corpus.

August 29, 2011

Imam Jamil's attorneys filed an appeal to the Georgia State Supreme Court challenging the habeas denial.

Imam Jamil remains incarcerated in Florence, Colorado, housed by the Federal Bureau of Prisons. The State of Georgia continues to pay a daily per diem rate to the Bureau of Prisons for his incarceration.

March 2013

A FOIA (Freedom Of Information Act) request is submitted to the FBI by Attorney Karima Al-Amin to produce documents on Imam Jamil. The FBI responded that it had identified and would produce 21,649 pages of records from more than 44,000 pages.

May 2013

Imam Jamil became ill, initially with a dental problem that quickly escalated into major medical problems.

June 2014

With the intervention of family members, attorneys, congressional representatives and the public, the Federal Bureau of Prisons conducted blood and other tests.

July 2014

After additional public pressure on the Federal Bureau of Prisons to stop the *"execution by medical neglect"* of Imam Jamil, the imam is moved out of the supermax prison in Florence, Colorado, to the federal Butner Medical Center, in North Carolina. Imam Jamil has a bone marrow biopsy that confirmed he has *smoldering myeloma,* an intermediate pre-cursor stage of *multiple myeloma* – a cancer of plasma cells.

October 2014

Imam Jamil is moved from the Butner Medical Center to the USP Canaan federal prison, in Waymart, PA, where for the first time since 2002 he was placed in general population. After 14 years of incarceration consisting of administrative and solitary confinement, Imam Jamil was able to attend religious services and events in general population.

September-October 2015

The FBI released the fourth Freedom of Information Act interim CD to Karima Al-Amin, which contained a BOLO ("Be On The Lookout") bulletin issued the day after the March 16, 2000 shootout, *with a description of the shooter of the sheriff's deputies that did not match Imam Jamil.* The newly disclosed FOIA documents were presented to the Court as a supplement to the habeas.

December 2015

Imam Jamil is moved from the USP Canaan federal prison to the USP Tucson, Arizona, federal prison – after he requested a move to a warmer climate closer to Atlanta, GA. Since the move is approximately 1,700 miles from his legal team, family, and supporters, he continued to request a suitable transfer.

November 18, 2016

Counsel from Kilpatrick, Townsend & Stockton argue Imam Jamil's federal habeas before a judge in the U.S. District Court for the

Northern District of Georgia. Constitutional issues are raised pertaining to the prosecutor's inflammatory and prejudicial closing argument that violated Imam Jamil's right not to testify. Other issues raised focused on the confession that was not presented at trial; and 911tapes that were also withheld from the jury.

May 3, 2019

Kilpatrick-Townsend attorneys present the oral argument before the 11th Circuit Court of Appeals to have the denial of the federal habeas overturned, primarily based on the egregious behavior of the trial prosecutor's closing argument that violated the imam's 5th Amendment right.

July 31, 2019

The 11th Circuit Court of Appeals affirms the federal district court's denial of the federal habeas petition. Attorneys decide to file a writ before the U.S. Supreme Court.

October 29, 2019

The Petition for Certiorari was filed in the U.S. Supreme Court challenging the 11th Circuit Court of Appeals affirmation of the denial of the federal habeas by the lower federal courts.

Imam Jamil remains in the USP Tucson federal prison while he maintains his innocence. Attempts continue to be made to monitor his health to ensure he is receiving proper medical care. Efforts also continue to garner support for the campaign to have Imam Jamil moved closer to Georgia where family, attorneys and supporters would have greater access to him.

A special note of thanks to Sr. Karima Al-Amin for providing a very informative chronological sketch on her husband of many years of hard-fought struggle.

Karima Al-Amin (Attorney-At-Law)

Sis. Karima Al-Amin is an attorney at law and the wife of political prisoner Imam Jamil Abdullah Al-Amin. In addition to her private practice, Mrs. Al-Amin continues to work with attorneys in appealing her husband's conviction and in working on his civil lawsuits challenging First Amendment and religious violations. Mrs. Al-Amin is a member of several legal and community organizations, including the American Immigration Lawyers Association (AILA), the Clarkston Business Association, and the Georgia Association of Muslim Lawyers (GAML).

CHAPTER 2 - H. Rap Brown & the 1968 Olympic Protest for Human Rights

This chapter reveals just how broad the influence of H. Rap Brown became beyond the realm of what was considered in the late 1960s "traditional civil rights advocacy." It also serves as a reminder to young activists of today that sports-related activism is nothing new!

An Interview with Dr. Harry Edwards

H. Rap Brown, John Carlos, Harry Edwards, Stokely Carmichael
Howard University, Washington, DC - October 1968

Preface

October 2018 marks the 50th anniversary of the historic and remarkable organizing initiative to boycott the 1968 Olympics in Mexico City. Dr. Harry Edwards led the boycott efforts, as well as the creation of the "Olympic Project for Human Rights" in which he involved countless Black activists from throughout the country, including H. Rap Brown.

On October 21, 2018, I [Heather Gray] was fortunate to interview Dr. Edwards about his 1968 organizing efforts and his affiliation with H. Rap Brown who also played a leading and inspirational role in this historic 1968 event. What follows is the transcription of my interview with Dr. Edwards.

H. Rap Brown later took the name Jamil Abdullah Al-Amin and, as a Muslim leader, was the influential imam in Atlanta's West End where he consistently attempted, among other missions, to end the drug invasion in the West End community. In 2000, an Atlanta policeman was killed, and Al-Amin was accused of this crime, yet all the indications are that he was not the killer. In fact, another individual, named Otis Jackson, confessed to being the shooter on the evening of March 16, 2000, and yet this was never introduced at trial by the prosecution or defense. Otis Jackson continues to maintain that he was the assailant.

When Jamil Al-Amin was first imprisoned in Atlanta for this alleged crime, I visited him briefly, along with Alabama attorney J.L. Chestnut, who had been defending Al-Amin while he was in Alabama just after the killing of the Atlanta policeman. During the 2002 trial that ended in the conviction of Jamil Al-Amin, we consistently held radio shows on WRFG-Atlanta, along with Al-Amin's brother Ed Brown, regarding updates of the trial. Many of us, including myself, were observers in the courtroom.

Al-Amin is now in the United States Prison (USP) in Tucson, Arizona where he is housed in the general population. He continues to declare his innocence, and supporters are advocating for his return to a Georgia facility where he will finally be able to receive regular visits from family and friends [and also have proximity to his attorneys].

At the end of the transcription is a brief biography of Dr. Edwards, as well as the listing of the four requests made to the Olympic Committee by the Olympic Project for Human Rights.

Harry Edwards: Let me talk about Rap and my motivation for bringing him into this situation. In 1964, when I graduated from San Jose State University, I had the options of going into the National Football League (NFL) draft, or the National Basketball Association (NBA) draft, or even sticking around and preparing for the '64 Olympics as I had thrown the discus far enough to qualify for the trials. But I had a Woodrow Wilson fellowship to Cornell University which, in point of fact, paid more. So that's the option that I took.

And while I was there, I wrote my Masters' thesis on the Black Muslim family. And some of the people that I interviewed were part of Malcolm X's group down in New York City. So, I became very much influenced after listening to Malcolm and really coming to understand the extent to which he had literally changed his perspective and paradigm relative to his analysis of African-American circumstances in this country.

And there were two points that he made that really stuck with me. The first was that we had to move from a focus on 'civil rights' to human rights, because that broadened our basis for not just protest but of alliance possibilities. Because, if we focus on civil rights, we're stuck within the context of the American judicial political system; but if we begin to talk about human rights, then that puts us on the same level and the same forum with other human beings on this earth.

First meeting of the Olympic Project for Human Rights: December 1967 San Jose State Tommie Smith, Lee Evans, Harry Edwards, James Edwards (Student Body President-elect) Note the drawings of H. Rap Brown on the wall

The second point that Malcolm made, so clearly, was that the extent to which we were going to be able to make any progress was going to be dependent upon the extent to which there was unity among those who were struggling in this country - especially African

American groups. Not "uniformity" but "unity." We could all be coming from different aspects of the struggle, but there had to be some unity in terms of how we projected that protest power.

And so, the notion of "human rights" led me to term the struggle in sports the *"Olympic Project for Human Rights."* And this notion of unity led me to try to broaden the bases of struggle. One of the key people in that whole process was H. Rap Brown.

Gold medalist Tommie Smith and bronze medalist John Carlos after the 200 m race at the 1968 Olympics; both wear Olympic Project for Human Rights badges. Peter Norman (silver medalist) from Australia also wears an OPHR badge in solidarity with Smith and Carlos.

If you recall back at that time, in 1967/68, Dr. (Martin Luther) King was on the outs with virtually everybody. The more impatient, younger, more militant people involved in the struggle had even started calling him the "Lawd" because he spoke and people responded, oftentimes, unquestioningly. But many young people were beginning to question both the non-violent method, as well as the goal of desegregation, that left Black communities literally stranded and isolated and devoid of their leadership structure.

Institutions within the Black community began to collapse, as the middle classes and higher levels of social economic order in American society, including Black society, began to move into and onto the periphery of institutions in the white society. So black restaurants, black hotels, black schools, black newspapers, and most certainly Blacks involved in sports, such as the Negro leagues - all of that began to collapse.

And so there was this young militant group moving into a new direction and a different paradigm than Dr. King. *And then the mainstream that had been so supportive of him, particularly the economic structures, and the unions and some liberal government interests, and even the other Black churches and pastors began to turn away from him because of his outspokenness about the Vietnam War.* They thought he had got out of his lane and was bringing undue pressure on the civil rights movement, and as a consequence, they were suffering as well as him. So they turned on him.

But Dr. King wanted to begin to pool these pieces back together. And so one of the things that I did was to get in touch with Dr. King, through my good friend Louis Lomax, and set up a meeting where we could talk about his endorsement possibilities of the Olympic Project for Human Rights. I also got in touch with Rap.

I had been working with Ralph Featherstone, in point of fact, since February to endorse the Olympic Project for Human Rights. So, my goal with the Olympic Project for Human Rights was to bring in SNCC [Student Non-Violent Coordinating Committee], to bring in the Black Panther Party, which I was a member of, and Huey Newton, Bobby Seale; to bring in Dr. King and Floyd McKissik - to bring in all of these interests around the Olympic Project for Human Rights.

The person, the catalyst in terms of the more militant youthful groups, was H. Rap Brown. Because Rap, at that point in 1968, was the chair of SNCC and probably the most militant face and profile of the younger Black movement in this country. So when he signed off on the boycott of the New York Athletic Club, when he signed off on the Olympic Project for Human Rights it made it possible for everybody else on that side of the civil rights divide to line up behind the movement.

And then, of course, when Dr. King signed off that brought in Floyd McKissick of the Congress of Racial Equality and a number of other groups who were more traditionally establishment civil rights leaders.

So Rap played a critical role in terms of bringing that unity that Malcolm had discussed, at least around this one issue of the Olympic Project for Human Rights. It was an important starting point I felt.

Harry Edwards and H. Rap Brown -February. 12, 1968, New York

I was involved with Rap, in point of fact, before he went to prison the first time, around the situation in New York City. I was a graduate student at Cornell University, and I would come down to New York City to do research and various other activities in the city and a lot of times Rap would pick me up at the airport. But he and James Forman and Stokely Carmichael were major factors in me framing up the possibilities in terms of political leverage, using sports to bring more people into a circle of understanding about what our obligations were.

We could not allow these athletes who had this tremendous forum...this tremendous megaphone...to simply stand out there and continually salute the flag as our churches were being bombed; as our leaders were being shot down; as our children and old Black women were being dribbled down the street like basketballs with firehoses that were so powerful they could take the bark off of trees. Athletes with that great forum had to stand up and say essentially, "We're better than this." And so, to galvanize people around that idea, people who had not seen sport in exactly that framework, was critical. And Rap was one of the early people - early on individuals - who understood that.

But, of course, Rap was an athlete himself. A lot of people think Kaepernick was the first Black quarterback to become politicized and to militantly assault racism and injustice in the American society. But the first Black quarterback to do that, *that I knew*, was H. Rap Brown, who had gone to Southern University on a scholarship before he joined SNCC, and began to really become active in the movement.

He was a heck of an athlete. Rap loved to play basketball, play football; he was in sports just like he was in life. He went out to win, to get things done. So he was the first Black quarterback that I knew who became actively involved in the movement and literally set sports aside so that he could do that.

Heather Gray: *Given all the activism all of you and others were engaged in, how is it expressed in today's world?*

Edwards: Well, first of all, the fact that 50 years after the Olympic Project for Human Rights, not only is it being talked about, it's actually being commemorated and celebrated all over the world. We just finished a program at San Jose State University where there's a 30-foot statue of Smith and Carlos on the campus. But there were people in from Germany, South Africa, Mexico - of course, Italy, France, Brazil...I mean there were people there from all over the world to cover it.

The program that we had was live streamed and if anyone is interested in looking at that program they can go to the San Jose University website and the entire program is up on that website.

Sports sociologist Harry Edwards and the Olympic Black Power Statue on the San Jose State University campus.
Photo: Santiago Mejia / The Chronicle

We had many of the people involved in that movement on the stage and involved in panels including John Carlos and Tommy Smith, and people like Spencer Haywood, and most certainly Wyomia Tyus, and others. So, they can go and look at that. But the fact that we're talking about it 50 years later means that it had an impact.

The thing with regard to H. Rap Brown was that, like Malcolm, Rap continued to evolve. He continued to evolve his knowledge and understanding, and so forth, of the movement and challenges that are involved. Most people have no idea of what happened to him after the 1960's. But Rap, of course, was a central figure of focus in J. Edward Hoover's COINTELPRO program, as was I, and Stokely Carmichael, and a lot of other people.

But he changed his name. Changed in terms of developing a religious focus. And a lot of people who knew him as H. Rap Brown kind of got lost in the trade winds of change and have no idea what happened to him or where he is today.

Heather Gray: *Why do you think H. Rap Brown changed?*

Edwards: Well, I think that we all change. The issue becomes whether we're developing in a positive direction. It's like I tell people about the whole notion of progress in society or in the struggle. Progress is one of those concepts that's a lot like profit. At one point it comes down to who's keeping the books. And it's the same with regard to individual development and progress. At some point it comes down to who's writing the biography. And if nothing is being written of it in bits and pieces, or nothing at all, you don't get the full story as to what is happening in a person's life or the impact that they might be having today as a consequence of the changes that have taken place. But we all change. The issue is whether our lives are being directed by us to the extent that that is possible, or whether our lives are something that is evolving while we're doing something else.

I think Rap was on top of the evolution in his life. I think he had a very good idea of the direction he was moving in and what he wanted to do. I think the discipline of Islam, and the very way that it allowed him to frame up increasingly more complicated developments, born as much of the successes of the 1960s, as of the failures. I think all of that propelled him in a different direction than where he was going when he was H. Rap Brown and chairman of SNCC.

***Heather Gray:** You have made reference to the fact that Nelson Mandela had a copy of the flier you all developed in 1968 for the Olympic event. Apparently, someone was able to smuggle that flier into his cell while he was imprisoned on Robben Island in South Africa. When I was in South Africa, a few years ago, I was able to visit Mandela's cell on Robben Island. I was also fortunate to be in South Africa when Mandela was inaugurated in 1994, and he had some of the white prison guards from Robben Island on the platform with him, because he had such a profound influence on everyone around him, including other inmates and the guards as well.*

Now, attorney J. L. Chestnut from Alabama, who was always assisting H. Rap Brown in the 1960's when Rap was arrested sometimes during the 60's movement, told me that the authorities in Alabama were always nervous about Rap when he was in prison. This is because he always had such a profound impact on the inmates and guards around him. That is still in effect today because the Federal Bureau of Prisons also gets really nervous about Jamil mixing too much with the general prison population, as well as with the guards. So it's on-going, Dr. Edwards?

Edwards: Absolutely. Of course, any time you have someone of that stature and that clarity of mind in terms of who they are, and what they are about, it becomes a threat to a system where the basic guideline is "control." And so, if they want to maintain maximum control, they do what they have done in this case, which is to eliminate all interview possibilities. It's virtually impossible to get a letter into Jamil in this situation. And it's one of the ways that the system controls people that it determines to be an on-going and palpable threat.

Paul Robeson - Culver Pictures

Heather Gray: *So, why are the government entities nervous about someone like Jamil Al-Amin?*

Edwards: Well, the problem that the system has is that it can allow an individual to be free and to speak, or they can lock him down, or her down, in total isolation and so forth. If they allow them to be free to speak and to organize and so forth, then they have a problem because there can be influence in that regard. And so you have these kinds of efforts to isolate and eliminate their legitimacy, as happened with Paul Robeson; as is happening now with Colin Kaepernick.

Or you can lock them down, but under those circumstances you create a martyr. So the only way that you can kind of slow down the martyrdom is to totally isolate this person - no contact, no discussion, no information. So then isolated, people will not know what's going on, what others are thinking, what they're doing; and over a period of time a person can become so isolated, so insulated, so incapsulated that they actually lose contact with the linguistic currency of the current era.

Colin Kaepernick taking the knee for justice – Time Sports

They can't even speak to people of the Gen Generation, or the X Generation, or the Boomerang Generation, or whatever they want to call the current group of young up and coming activists. They lose contact. They lose access to the linguistic currency necessary to communicate with them; and that's the hope of the system. That's what total isolation can do where they control your reading materials; what you can listen to on the radio or watch on the television set; they control who can send you letters; they control letters you can send out. And the next thing you know, somebody who has been isolated has lost touch and contact with the broader masses of people who they would influence, and who would benefit from their wisdom and knowledge.

So, that is the kind of struggle that takes place when you have somebody like Jamil in this kind of a total lockdown set of circumstances.

Heather Gray: *So, I guess the assumption is basically that the powers that be, whether it's J. Edgar Hoover, the CIA, COINTELPRO, or the present United States government overall, they want to continue* *this oppression of people. They want to be able to control them the way they want.*

Edwards: Absolutely. And even in the age of the internet and social media, there is still concern about the management of information; and that becomes a real challenge for anyone who they would oppress today. They can lock an individual down - that takes place - but more in the boarder spectrum of things, since they can't totally manage information in the age of social media and the internet, there's a reliance on fake information.

[*Editor's note: Case in point is the Wikipedia on Dr. Aafia Siddiqui. It has been so successful in demonizing the victim, that potential supporters have been frightened away. The same has happened to Imam Jamil. A vivid example of the negative power of malicious propaganda!]

We have a president who is a pathological liar - a morally malignant degenerate - but he continues to put out this information that paints everybody else as fake, and lying, and so forth. So that's what they've been driven to in this age as the consequence of social media. But where they can, they will lock people down, isolate them, cut them off. And, unfortunately, that's what's happening to Jamil.

Heather Gray: What can we share with others, what can be inspirational as far as learning more about Jamil and his impact on the United States, and on the world, as far as international justice is concerned. How would you summarize that? What would you tell the people about him to learn from him and be inspired?

El-Hajj Malik El-Shabazz (Malcolm X)

Edwards: The first thing that I would tell them is to follow the direction of Malcolm X. Malcolm said the reading and study of history is the greatest of all endeavors because it allows you to frame up how we got to where we are. I would have them go online - one of the great benefits of social media - and dig up everything they possible could about H. Rap Brown, and about the man that he evolved into [Imam Jamil Abdullah Al-Amin].

The second thing that I would suggest is that people understand something that Rap Brown told me over half a century ago; and that is there are no messiahs, because individuals never survive - only the people and the struggle survive.

And a point that he made is something that I continue to reiterate, and that is that there are no final victories. Not only should we not be looking for a messiah, who has all of the answers and who's going to lead us out of this wilderness, but there are no final victories. It is going to be up to every generation to fight their battles, and not just because they're the battles they are confronted with. But if they do not, then the next generation will not only have to fight its battles, but it will have to fight the battles that the previous generation should have fought.

And never ever get into a frame of mind where you think that because you have won a battle, that somehow that is permanent and unchanging. We are fighting now voter suppression on the face of having achieved the Voting Rights Act; we're dealing with medical services for women in the face of having achieved Roe v Wade; and all these other things. We are going back and again battling over a terrain that many people thought was conquered.

So, there are no final victories. There are no messiahs. There are just those who are committed to fighting the battle, and I think that is what H. Rap Brown and his evolution is indicative of.

Dr. King's anti-Vietnam War Speech at Riverside Church – 1967

I watched Malcolm X - he evolved. I watched Dr. King evolve. In the end he was talking about economic development. He died in the struggle for economic development in Memphis. He was talking about anti-war measures. I watched Dr. King evolve.

So, everybody has to evolve not just in generational terms, but individually. That's the model. That's the lesson we can learn from studying the life of H. Rap Brown and the individual, the man who he evolved into.

***Heather Gray:** One of the things that, in the movement, people were evolving to engage in was "human rights." Could you please explain that again? What specifically is human rights?*

Edwards: As long as we were talking about civil rights, if it was on the books, it was done. Then it comes down to going down to vote. Then it comes down to going out to buying a home. Then it comes down to going to this school rather than the school that you were restricted to. That's civil rights.

Human rights has to do with the respect and dignity of the individual. It goes beyond civil rights. It goes to the issue of having the right to live and walk on this earth with the dignity of a human being. So this comes down to being able to have safety in your home. Being able to have nutritional necessities met.

I was speaking at a campus this week where students regularly have to choose between books and breakfast, in the richest country on earth.

- Being able to have nutritional security in America should be a human right.
- Health care should be a human right.
- Being able to walk the streets of any community in this country should be a human right.
- It is not a matter of civil rights that 147 Black men, women and children are summarily executed in the streets of this country every year by police. That's an issue of human rights.

Harry Edwards - circa 1967

And so, the issue of human rights, as Malcolm X pointed out as early as 1964, goes beyond what's on the books in terms of civil rights. It goes down to the dignity and respect and stature of a human being, on this planet, in this country, at this time...and so the impact of the struggle for human rights encompasses civil rights, but it goes so much beyond that. And it involves all groups.

When we talk about civil rights we tend to talk about "Black" civil rights. Black right to vote. Black right to housing equity. Black right to healthcare.

When we talk about human rights, we're talking about women, we're talking about students on campuses across this country. We're talking about old folks and their right to live out their lives in dignity, and so forth. We're talking about women's rights to hold a job without being sexually harassed and being able to walk the streets without feeling threatened in their very person because they are women.

When we are talking about human rights, we are talking about the fact that a lot of what happens to black women doesn't happen to them because they are black, it happens to them because they are women. And that's a human concern that we have to have.

And so, I think that when we talk about human rights, when we expand our struggle - as we tried to do with the Olympic Project for Human Rights in 1968 - that Rap Brown was so much a part of in bringing in the militant youth movement, in alliance with Dr. King and Floyd McKissick, and the Congress of Racial Equality, we're talking about where we need to go with the movement in this country. And it also ties into something that James Baldwin said.

James Baldwin wrote a book in 1962 called <u>The Fire Next Time</u>. In there he said, "We must be visionary enough, we must have the will, and we must have the wisdom to include everybody in our strategies for change because, to the extent that we do not, then we are once again destined to fulfill those words from the Bible, put to song

56

by a slave, *'God gave Noah the rainbow sign. No more water. The fire next time.'"*

And because the movement that had been established in the civil rights movement, left so many Black people behind in places like Watts and the southside of Chicago, and so forth... Baldwin wrote that book in 1962 and in 1965, Watts exploded.

So we have to understand that we now have to begin to talk about human rights, as Rap Brown did fifty years ago...as the Olympic Project on Human Rights focused on fifty years ago...as Malcolm X spoke of *over* fifty years ago...as Dr. King was moving toward when he started talking about economic rights and the war in Vietnam, and so forth, fifty years ago.

So that struggle continues. And the individual that was Rap Brown, who is now Jamil Al-Amin, is as much at the center of that struggle today as he was then.

***Heather Gray**: Dr. Harry Edwards, I want to thank you so much. And as the South Africans always say "Aluta continua" - the struggle continues - which is what you are saying as well.*

Edwards: Absolutely!

About Dr. Harry Edwards

Sociology professor and civic activist Harry Edwards was born in 1942 in East St. Louis, Illinois, to Harry and Adelaide Edwards. Edwards grew up in East St. Louis as the second child in a family of eight children. He attended the newly integrated East St. Louis Senior High School where he excelled in sports.

After graduating from high school in 1960, Edwards moved to California where he attended Fresno City College. Edwards then transferred to San Jose State University where he majored in sociology and graduated summa cum laude with his B.A. degree in sociology in 1964. In 1966, Edwards went on to receive his M.A. degree in sociology from Cornell University where he was awarded the Woodrow Wilson Fellowship.

In 1970, he received his Ph.D. degree in sociology from Cornell University where he helped to found United Black Students for Action and the Olympic Project for Human Rights.

Due to his negative experiences as a student athlete on predominately white university campuses, Edwards became heavily involved in exposing the relationship between race and sports in society. By the late 1960s, Edwards began actively organizing protests and demonstrations like the 1968 Olympics Black Power salute at Mexico City involving John Carlos, Peter Norman and Tommie Smith. (The History Makers)

Four Central Demands of OPHR

- Restore Muhammad Ali's heavyweight boxing title.
- Remove Avery Brundage as head of the International Olympic Committee (IOC).
- Hire more African American coaches.
- Disinvite Apartheid South Africa and Rhodesia from the Olympics.

Ali was stripped of his heavyweight title earlier in the year for his resistance to the Vietnam draft. By standing with Ali, OPHR was expressing its opposition to the war. By calling for the hiring of more

African American coaches as well as the ouster of Brundage, they were dragging out of the shadows a part of Olympic history those in power wanted to bury.

Brundage was an anti-Semite and a white supremacist, best remembered today for sealing the deal on Hitler's hosting the 1936 Olympics in Berlin. By demanding the exclusion of South Africa and Rhodesia, they aimed to convey their internationalism and solidarity with the black freedom struggles against apartheid in Africa

CHAPTER 3 - THE TARGETING CONTINUES

Special note: In this chapter we explore the case of Imam Jamil stemming from the tragic events of March 16, 2000. Also included in this chapter is the written advice offered by the late Coretta Scott King in the opening days of the trial. Advice, it should be noted, that she was roundly criticized for from certain quarters of the establishment.

The Demands of Revolutionary Struggle

"I knew I could never again raise my voice against the violence of the oppressed in the ghettos without having first spoken clearly to the greatest purveyor of violence in the world today – my own government."

These were the words of one of 20th century America's most courageous champions for freedom, the Rev. Dr. Martin Luther King, Jr. America's leading advocate of creative non-violence made this observation on April 4, 1967, in a speech variously known as *"Beyond Vietnam,"* and *"A Time to Break the Silence,"* delivered at Riverside Church in New York City.

According to Dr. King, young black men began to point out the contradictions of the anti-violence campaign in the civil rights movement when contrasted against the government's violent campaigns in Vietnam. One of those "young black men" was H. Rap Brown, the man known throughout America today as Imam Jamil Abdullah Al-Amin.

Many years later when Imam Jamil was in the Washington, DC, area for a speaking engagement at the University of Maryland, I had the pleasure of driving him to the airport for his return home the following day. Enroute to the airport I asked a question that I could only ask of someone who was one of the most prominent surviving activists of the 1960s movement: "What was it like, Brother Imam…the African American struggle for human rights during the 60s?" I'll never forget his response. Without the slightest hesitation he noted, *"It was a war."* (Some wars never end.)

While some have argued that Imam Jamil lost his revolutionary edge when he embraced Islam – as one observer put it, "He went from revolution to religious rhetoric" – nothing could be further from the truth. As the essential meaning of the word revolution denotes "a complete change," those of us who know him well would counter that with his embrace of Islam, H. Rap Brown became a true revolutionary in the fullest sense of the word. His maturity as an agent for positive change deepened.

In his book entitled, <u>Revolution By The Book</u> (published by Writer's Inc., 1994) he writes: "It is criminal that, in the 1990s, we still approach struggle [by] sloganeering, saying, `By any means necessary,' as if that's a program, or `We shall overcome,' as if that's a program. Slogans are not programs. We must define the means which will bring about change. This can be found in what Allah has brought for us in the Qur'an and in the example of the Prophet. Our revolution must be according to what Almighty God revealed...

"The mission of a believer in Islam is totally different from coexisting or being a part of the system. The prevailing morals are wrong; their ethics are wrong. Western philosophy has reduced man to food, clothing, shelter, and the sex drive, which means he doesn't have a spirit...Successful struggle requires a divine program. Allah has provided that program."

The Night of March 16, 2000

"We've got a blood trail leading into a [vacant] house."
"Be advised that…the subject is gonna be bleeding…"
"Radio to all units…a blood trail."
(Police radio transmissions the night of March 16th)

It was the month of Dhul Hijjah, 1420 AH, on the eve of one of
the two most important holidays in the Muslim calendar, Eid ul-Adha
(corresponding with the date March 16, 2000 CE). Muslim pilgrims
from around the world were completing the last rites of Hajj, the
pilgrimage to Makkah (an occasion so sacred that it is forbidden to
even kill an insect while in pilgrim garb). Muslim families throughout
America were preparing for the festive Eid celebration which comes at
the end of this religious rite.

This was the backdrop for the shootout which occurred on the
West End of Atlanta. Far from being your ordinary urban pathology,
the reverberations of this particular shootout would echo around
America and make headline news in other parts of the world. At its
conclusion, two Fulton County sheriff's deputies would lay critically
wounded, and a nationwide alert would be issued for a wounded "ex-
Black Panther," identified as "the former H. Rap Brown," a man
known and respected throughout much of America's Muslim
community and beyond as Imam Jamil Abdullah Al-Amin.

Both deputies, Ricky Kinchen (who would succumb to his injuries the following day) and Aldranon English claimed to have wounded the assailant in the stomach area, and media reports described a blood trail leading into an abandoned house. Shortly after the deadly encounter a 911 emergency caller reported a bleeding man a few blocks away begging motorists for a ride. When Imam Jamil was taken into custody four days later in a little town call White Hall, Alabama, authorities were shocked to learn he had no injuries.

Approximately one year later, during a motions hearing in the case, a courtroom full of observers would be stunned by a police official's sworn testimony that, *"There was no blood...there never was any blood...we made a mistake."*

A Statement from the Accused

My name is Imam Jamil Abdullah Al-Amin, the former H. Rap Brown. I am a devoted servant of ALLAH, and an unwavering devotee to His cause. For more than 30 years I have been tormented and persecuted by my enemies for reasons of race and belief. I seek truth over a lie; I seek justice over injustice; I seek righteousness over the rewards of evildoers, and I love ALLAH more than I love the state.

"Their intention is to extinguish ALLAH'S light (by blowing) with their mouths; but ALLAH will complete (the revelation of) His light, even though the unbelievers may detest it." Qur'an 61:8

On March 16, 2000, Fulton County Sheriff Deputy Ricky Kinchen was killed and Sheriff Aldranon English was shot and injured in the neighborhood where I have lived, worked, and prayed. Indeed, this tragedy occurred across the street from the Mosque I founded.

I have been accused by the State of Georgia of having committed these crimes. Let me declare before the FAMILIES of these men, before the STATE, and ANYONE who would care to know the truth, that I am INNOCENT of the 13 charges that have been brought against me. Let me also declare that I am joined at the heart with his widow and her children at the loss of a husband and father. I drink from the same bitter cup of sorrow as the siblings at the loss of a beloved brother. I am powerless to do anything to ease your pain and suffering except pray that ALLAH comforts you in your hour of need and grant you peace for the remainder of your days.

I have been maliciously maligned, scandalized and vilified in the press by the police establishment before the court of world opinion, even before I was charged with any crime. They have sought to marginalize my humanity and humiliate my family. They have done their level best to reduce me to a one-dimensional monster that is a composite of a Black Panther with a negative connotation, a cop killer, and the fictional character of the Godfather. I am entitled to every right and every consideration as every other human being, including fairness, a fair trial, and the presumption of innocence.

Fulton County District Attorney, Paul Howard, as a representative of the state has asked for my death. Mr. Howard can have my death based on the power of the state, but not on the basis of justice. He can only have my death because my life belongs to ALLAH, and He alone in life and in death will deliver me from my tormentors and persecutors. I will pray for those who spitefully abuse me because of power, prestige or blind ambition; for they must face the ultimate bar of justice and face the Judge of Judges and answer the question: `By what right and whose permission did you ask for death of this human being, and my devoted servant?'

Statement from Mrs. Coretta Scott King

I want to express my concern about fairness and justice in the trial of Mr. Jamil Abdullah Al-Amin, who is accused in the murder of Deputy Ricky Kinchen and the shooting of Deputy Aldranon English.

While I well understand the need for swift and decisive justice, especially on behalf of the victims' families, who have suffered so much, I feel that it is critically important that the rights of the accused be fully respected and protected at every phase of this trial. All of the inconsistencies that have emerged in this case must be thoroughly explored and fully investigated, and a clear and unequivocal motive must be established for the verdict to have the credibility needed for closure.

Mr. Jamil Abdullah Al-Amin is entitled to the same presumption of innocence until proven guilty, and impartial justice that is the birthright of every citizen. For justice to be faithfully served, there must be no rush to judgment and the defense must be allowed to present all of its evidence, just as the prosecution must uphold the highest standards in meeting the burden of proof.

This terrible tragedy has already caused much pain and suffering among the loved ones of the victims, and indeed for all who care about the safety of the public servants who protect

*our community. This tragedy must not be compounded by a
flawed trial or rushed verdict. All care must be taken to insure
that justice prevails for the victims, the defendant, and the
community. If these standards are scrupulously observed and
reflected in the outcome, then the healing process can begin.*
[End of statement]

It is worth noting here that, just as her husband was widely
vilified after delivering his "Beyond Vietnam" speech in 1967, she too
was publicly criticized for "interfering" in the case of Imam Jamil (for
simply calling for a fair and just proceeding).

In the following pages, we will do our best to provide a concise
and comprehensive, yet substantive snapshot on the case that media
organizations and law enforcement agencies throughout the US
followed closely from start to finish; but chose to limit detailed
exposure of during the trial phase. The question is…why?

Even **Court TV**, after initially expressing a keen interest in
broadcasting the trial, decided in the 11th hour to not cover it. The
reason given for the abrupt reversal was the stated belief that there was
"diminished public interest" - because Jamil Abdullah Al-Amin had
changed his name from H. Rap Brown. (*"Diminished public interest"*
despite the carefully managed attention the case would receive
nationwide. Court TV chose to broadcast a dog mauling trial instead.
So much for "public interest.")

The Government's Case

The government's case against Imam Jamil was predicated on the
following:

(1) The eyewitness testimony of the surviving deputy, Aldranon
English;

(2) The fact that both deputies were on the West End of Atlanta to serve a warrant for Imam Jamil's arrest;

(3) Officers who arrived at the scene acquired a description of the shooter from both Kinchen and English that reportedly matched the defendant (this has been a matter of contention);

(4) Imam Jamil fled the Atlanta area and became a fugitive;

(5) When apprehended four days later in Lowndes County, Alabama, in a little town known as White Hall, he reportedly had a passport in his possession, $1,000 in cash, and was wearing body armor (a bullet proof vest);

(6) Imam Jamil is alleged to have fired shots at law enforcement officers on the night of his arrest;

(7) An automatic pistol, assault rifle, three spent shell casings and two .223 caliber magazine casings (taped together) were reportedly recovered from the wooded area from which Imam Jamil emerged on the night of his arrest. Ballistics tests would allegedly tie this "evidence" to the March 16th crime in Atlanta;

(8) A black 1978 bullet-riddled Mercedes Benz, registered to Imam Jamil, was reportedly recovered in White Hall (AL) days later;

(9) Prosecutor McBirney's assertion in closing arguments: "I can't suggest to you that the state has answers for every single question… Where was the defendant at 10 pm on March 16? They had an opportunity to call witnesses to corroborate where he was – and that he wasn't there [at the crime scene] – but they didn't."

The Defense's Case

Imam Jamil's defense attorneys based their case on the following:

1) Defense counsel Martin's assertion that, "A fundamental mistake was made by layers of law enforcement when the assumption was made that they had their man [Imam Jamil];

the impartial investigation that should have ensued was never done."

2) The government had been pursuing Imam Jamil for a long time. The incident in Cobb County (GA) in September 1999 began the process for a "bogus indictment," which became the basis for a warrant "that never should have been issued."

3) The surviving eyewitness (Deputy English) was inconsistent in his description of the assailant and refused to be interviewed by defense attorneys all the way up to the time of the trial. The defense had to rely on his accounts given to state investigators.

4) Deputy English identified Imam Jamil from what the defense characterized as "a contaminated" photo spread only hours following the incident, and after being given four milligrams of morphine. The defense contended that he was in such a hallucinogenic state that English imagined being visited by several people standing around his hospital bed who were never there.

5) Both deputies insisted that they shot the assailant in the stomach area, and Deputy English maintained throughout that the assailant had grey eyes. (Imam Jamil's eyes are brown.)

6) Over time the long black trench like coat (or Islamic robe) became a long yellowish colored garment; and the grey eyes were adorned with yellowish tinted glasses.

7) The bullet-riddled squad car that was parked on the street at the time of the shootout, also hit by gunfire, was sold at auction before it could be examined by defense experts.

8) A car that was parked on the street at the time of the shootout, also hit by gunfire, was sold at auction before it could be examined by defense experts.

9) The physical evidence at the crime scene (i.e., position of shell casings) did not match English's account of the incident.

10) A law enforcement officer by the name of Sgt. Weaver reportedly found large droppings of blood at the crime scene, leading to an abandoned house.

11) The 911 emergency call concerning a bleeding person who pleaded with motorists for a ride, about a half a mile away from the crime scene.
12) A number of West End witnesses whose testimony pointed to someone other than Imam Jamil as the assailant.
13) Federal law enforcement personnel lied about what happened during the course of Imam Jamil's arrest. In the words of lead defense attorney Jack Martin, "reasoned logic would suggest that they would also lie about far more important matters."
14) "|Big John," a local sheriff's deputy, along with two other black officers, reportedly spotted Imam Jamil and ordered him to lay on the ground, where he was subsequently handcuffed behind his back. A white FBI agent (Ron Campbell) would arrive on the scene and proceed to kick Imam Jamil and spit on him, while he lay handcuffed on the ground.
15) Finally, Imam Jamil had no injuries; there was no damage to the vest he was wearing, no fingerprints on the guns, and no evidence of gunshot residue on his person on the night of his arrest. It has been suggested that evidence was planted in Alabama to insure a conviction of Imam Jamil.

The Otis Jackson Factor

According to the official record, a confession by a young man by the name of Otis Milton Jackson was formally given to investigators on or about June 29, 2000. Jackson reportedly signed a "Waiver of Rights," before being questioned on 6/29/00 at 2:15pm, in Las Vegas, Nevada. According to the identification sheet attached to his file, Jackson stood 6.8, weighed 165lbs. In the photo that accompanied his file, he appeared to be medium to dark complexioned, bald, with a short beard. (Jackson is not that tall. As I recall when I met him, he stood around 5.9/5.10)

Before examining Mr. Jackson's written affidavit, there are a number of other things worthy of note. According to the documentation, when Jackson "absconded supervision" and was extradited back to Nevada on Aril 13, 2000, as he was being booked into the Clark County Detention Center, "Jackson disclosed to the intake officer that he had been involved in a shooting/murder of an officer when he was in Georgia."

The amazing thing is what follows. The document reads: *"The detention officer did not investigate the statement. Inmate Jackson has been returned to the Nevada Department of Prisons, and presently he is undergoing intake processing. It would be greatly appreciated if you would investigate Jackson's assertion of involvement in a shooting/murder."*

The date on this State of Nevada Department of Corrections Memorandum is July 24, 2000, more than three months after Jackson made the confession of involvement in the death of a law enforcement officer! The memo was directed to a Sgt. Bennett of the Atlanta (GA) Police Department; an FBI interview of Jackson had already begun by June 29, 2000.

Another document ("Investigative Summary") issued by Senior Investigator Alvin M. Winston, of the Fulton County district Attorney's Office, Major Case Division, states that on July 2 (three days after the Nevada memorandum), Winston placed a call to the South Metro Parole Center to speak with Parole Officer Sarah Bacon about Otis Jackson. However, Parole Officer Tammy Pritchard informed Winston that Bacon was no longer an employee in the office and that Jackson's case had been transferred to the State of Nevada.

The obvious question is – if we accept this official paper trail on its face - why did it take Nevada authorities so long to contact Georgian authorities with a request to investigate a man who claimed to have been involved in the shooting of two Georgia law enforcement officers? And bear in mind, the March 16th tragedy made national headlines!

The Confession

The FBI summary that we have in our possession is signed off on by special agents Devon P. Mahoney and Lawrence K. Wenk[e], and appears to be based upon an investigation conducted on June 29, 2000; an interview of Jackson in the presence of Las Vegas Metropolitan Police Department Officers Dante Tromba and Greg Neglich. The things that stand out for me are the following quotes from the FBI summary report:

(1) "Jackson explained that he and Al-Amin were not friends but acquaintances."

(2) "Another black male was at the residence also waiting for Al-Amin."

(3) "Approximately 10 minutes after Jackson arrived at Al-Amin's residence, Al-Amin arrived. As the three men were talking, a police car arrived, and two police officers attempted to serve Al-Amin with a warrant."

(4) "Jackson then began fighting with Kinchen's partner and Kinchen came over to assist in the fight. Kinchen grabbed Jackson and Jackson stated that he spun out of Kinchen's grasp and then punched Kinchen in the face. Jackson then stated that he drew a 9mm Smith and Wesson from his pants waist band which was covered by his black Islamic robe. Jackson fired one shot at Kinchen and Jackson thought the round hit Kinchen in the stomach. Jackson immediately went to his car's trunk where Jackson had an SKS assault rifle, an M-16 machine gun, and a mini 14."

(5) "Kinchen's partner began to run away toward the main street…"

(6) "Jackson was able to shoot the retreating officer in the leg."

(7) "Jackson stated that during the shooting Al-Amin tried to stop Jackson from shooting at the officers by getting in Jackson's way. Al-Amin asked Jackson why he had shot the officers, but Jackson did not answer except to say that he was going home. Jackson stated that he thought the

other black male had been wounded because Jackson saw him lying on the street, but Jackson was not sure."
(8) "Jackson then left in his 1981 or 1982 Chevy Caprice Classic."
(9) "Jackson was asked (by investigators) why he shot at the officers. Jackson advised that he did not think the warrants for Al-Amin were valid, and he also did not like police. Jackson was asked why the police believed Al-Amin shot the officers. Jackson stated that he felt the officer made a mistake, since all three of the people there were black men with bald heads."

Officer Tromba, who reportedly witnessed the FBI interrogation of Jackson, stated in a July 13, 2000 debriefing, that while escorting Jackson back to his cell he commented, "Jackson's story was good except that he smiled too much." And further, "Jackson's people were going to owe Jackson in a big way."

Two things are evident from this statement: (1) Tromba – and probably most of the other investigating authorities – found Jackson's narration of the March 16 incident credible; (2) despite Jackson's believability, there appears to have been an immediate impulse to discredit him. The question is why?

The Recantation

Otis Jackson recanted his confession in a handwritten letter addressed to [then] U.S. Attorney General Janet Reno, within days of the June 29th confession. The things that stand out in this statement are the following:

(1) After identifying himself, he makes the following complaint: "I have been put on maximum custody at the Clark County Detention Center in Las Vegas, and they are charging me with the death of the deputy."
(2) The law enforcement people here are calling me cop killer, I don't want to eat or anything…If I'm not

charged then I would like to be put back in general
housing, and if I am charged then Atlanta needs to
come get me and not let me do my parole violation."

(3) Then he rails against the injustice that was committed
by the State of Texas against Gary Graham (aka Shaka
Sankofa) – a high profile political execution that took
place the previous year.

(4) He also states, "Vegas is giving me a case that I don't
have…Mr. Al-Amin nor myself did anything."

The final statement reads: "I, Otis Milton Jackson, was trying to
help a brother not knowing that it would give me the case. I love Jamil
but I did not do anything. I killed no one and Jamil killed no one. I'm
sorry for making the FBI feel as if I did this."

Is it conceivable that any man in his right mind would freely
confess to a serious crime without an awareness that his confession
will then result in him being charged with that crime? It is clear to me
that Jackson was/is psychologically unstable; and that his letter of
recantation to Reno was written under a great deal of duress.

Jackson was placed in maximum security and labeled a "cop
killer." Two of the worst labels any inmate can be incarcerated with
are child molester or child killer, and cop killer. In the former your
security is threatened by fellow inmates; in the latter your security can
be jeopardized by rogue correctional officers.

It is worth noting that attached to Jackson's file was a confidential
report, which suggested that after being transferred to maximum
security custody, Jackson came under heightened surveillance in order
to monitor any marked changes in his behavior. Among the signs that
came under close scrutiny – "any indication of suicidal tendencies."
(This document is dated July 10, 2000.)

The Confession Revisited

Not long after Imam Jamil's 2002 conviction, a long-time friend,
and highly regarded Muslim chaplain in the state of Georgia. Imam

Furqan Muhammad, brought to my attention a chance encounter he had with an inmate at the Gwinnett County Detention Center. As the chaplain described it: "One of the inmates gave me a sheet of notebook paper folded in half – not telling me what it was – just gave it to me. So as they were signing the attendance sheet, I decided to look at it. It read, 'I am Otis Jackson. I have confessed to the shooting of these two deputies, and I know that Imam Jamil is innocent, and I don't want an innocent man to go to jail for something that I did.'"

Jackson would go on to inform Imam Muhammad (and later this writer) that early on in the case he was interviewed twice by the FBI; once in Nevada and again in Atlanta. He said the FBI in Nevada didn't believe him, but the FBI in Atlanta did; because (according to him) much of what he had to say ran parallel to what actually occurred on the night of March 16, 2000. Jackson also stated that Fulton County District Attorney Paul Howard chose to discount him, telling FBI investigators they had the right man, referring to Imam Jamil, and didn't need Jackson "for nothing."

[* I can imagine the look on District Attorney Paul Howard's face upon hearing Ambassador Andrew Young's public declaration of his belief in Imam Jamil's innocence, at that January 2020 Fulton County DA Office's special event at Tyler Perry's Studios!]

The following is Otis Jackson's notarized statement to Imam Furqan A. Muhammad, dated March 14, 2002. (Jackson, a deeply troubled man with a troubled personal history, reportedly embraced Islam.)

I bear witness that there is no god but Allah, and I bear witness that Mohammed is the Messenger of Allah. I greet you in the greeting words of peace, As Salaam Alaikum.

My Dear Brother Furqan:

I respect you dearly, that's why I am writing this letter. In the Mirror International [newspaper] they say that they had a CNN report that said I, Otis Jackson, gave a confession to the shootings in the West End, then they say I recanted the confession. Brother, the District Attorney's office knows that Jamil did not do any shooting, and Deputy Aldranon English knows that Jamil did not shoot him. I asked them, the District Attorney, to show Mr. English my picture because I know that he would remember me. I am not a big fan of Imam Jamil Al-Amin but cannot sit back and let him take this case, and I know that Jamil did nothing. Imam Furqan, I should go to trial soon on this [present] case, and as soon as I get out, I give my word to Allah, I am going to free Imam Jamil. Brother, I pray the forgiveness of Allah and the Muslims.

Subsequent to this readmission, I personally visited Otis Jackson at the Gwinnett County Jail on May 9, 2002, and conducted my own interview. He is a young man, slightly built, who stands about 5ft 9 inches in height (not 6 ft. 8, as stated in the FBI report) and smiles easily. On the evening that I visited him at the Gwinnett County Jail, he was already aware of my pending arrival, and spoke easily about the tragic events of March 16, 2000, and their equally tragic aftermath.

For the sake of accuracy, it should also be noted that Otis Jackson carries a lot of unfortunate baggage in terms of credibility. I suspect this is the reason why Imam Jamil's defense team decided not to subpoena him as a witness during the trial in Georgia; and while I understand the reasoning, I disagree with that decision. Could he have been of value despite his tainted character and instability? This question will probably be debated for some time to come. With that said, it is this writer's humble opinion that Jackson's confession will carry considerable weight in the court of public opinion, if nowhere else.

My Interview of Otis Jackson at the Gwinnett County Jail - May 9, 2002

"I felt bad. I didn't know what he did in the past, but I know he didn't do this." – Otis Jackson

Otis Jackson stated on the day of the incident (March 16, 2000) he got off work sometime in the afternoon, when normally he would not leave until 11pm. He said he went straight from work to the West End Mall and remained until it was in the process of closing for the day (about 9pm). After leaving the Mall he said he stopped by "a Muslim brother's shop" on Ralph David Abernathy Blvd (next to the Shrine of the Black Madonna). The proprietor and his wife were just leaving when Jackson arrived, consequently he was asked to come back the following day.

He said he then proceeded to the area of West End Place near the masjid and saw a couple of brothers walking along the street, and another brother standing on the corner as if he were waiting for someone. He got into a conversation with the brother on the corner, and this went on until the drama unfolded with the arrival of the two Sheriff's Deputies.

With the exception of: (a) there being no mention of the arrival of Imam Jamil in this narration; (b) reference made to a wounded man being transported after the gun fight; (c) and the mysterious car that reportedly entered the intersection and sped off during the course of the gun fight - the remainder of his description of the tragedy corresponds with what was given to FBI investigators on June 29, 2000, before recantation.

Jackson provided me with the following narrative of what allegedly took place the night of the tragedy:

On March 16-18 he was "late reporting in" under the terms of his electronic monitoring agreement. He stated that on March 16th following the gunfight he went to another location to change his clothes, and then proceeded to drive a wounded brother to Macon,

Georgia. He also stated that when he went to the office of his parole officer on March 20th or 21st, he paid his customary $100 monitoring fee and was then informed by his parole officer that she would have to accompany him home as a consequence of his violation of the monitoring agreement.

When he and his parole officer arrived at his house, officers with the Atlanta Police Department were already present, and they informed him that they would have to do a search of the premises. According to Jackson, officers searched the premises and found 9 mm ammunition, AK47 ammunition, and 12-gauge shotgun shells. Jackson was placed under arrest for violating his parole, and soon after was sent back to the State of Nevada. Upon his arrival, he informed Nevada authorities of the shootout in Georgia.

When it appeared he was getting nowhere with his admission of guilt to Las Vegas authorities, Jackson said he placed a call to the office of the FBI (I'm assuming in Las Vegas); about two weeks later three agents visited him and conducted an interview. He informed me that subsequent to this visit, he would also receive a visit from an agent out of the Atlanta office.

Following his interview by FBI agents and Nevada police, he was placed in the 'hole," otherwise known as solitary confinement, at the Las Vegas Detention Center for approximately 30 days. While in solitary Jackson said he was publicly berated by some of the officers as a "cop killer," and felt coerced and threatened in other ways as well. He became suspicious of his food, and was advised by one or more officers, "Why don't you just tell them what they want you to say?"

He decided to recant his confession, under obvious emotional duress in a letter to [then]U.S. Attorney General Janet Reno. This came at the end of his first week in solitary confinement. He was later transferred to Indian Springs for 30 days (remaining in solitary there as well); and then onto High Desert State Prison for about six months in the general population. He also stated that at the time he recanted he believed there was no way Imam Jamil would be convicted for something he did not do.

When I asked Otis Jackson if he followed the trial of Imam Jamil, he responded no, he did not, because the circumstance of his confinement didn't allow him to follow the news. He said he learned about the conviction from Imam Furqan Muhammad on March 7th (in Georgia) - in comments made during the course of a session of Islamic services at the jail. The following week (March 14th), on the occasion of Imam Furqan's next visit, Jackson presented him with the note that opened with, **"My name is Otis Jackson…"** When I asked Jackson to relate how he felt upon hearing of the conviction of Imam Jamil, he responded: *"I felt bad. I didn't know what he did in the past, but I know he didn't do this."*

Facts and Inconsistencies

In the immediate aftermath of the March 16th tragedy many conflicting and contradictory reports were disseminated by the mainstream media (both print and broadcast); but as the dust settled, and certain facts began to emerge, a more accurate picture of the tragedy took shape. Jackson's confession is consistent with many of the known facts.

While the earliest reports had the assailant using only a .223 caliber assault rifle that was pulled from under a "black trench coat" (and one of the most commonly available .223 caliber weapons is the Ruger Mini-14), it soon became an established fact that a 9mm was also used by the assailant. Deputy Kinchen was reportedly shot in the abdomen and leg and died the following day. Deputy English (reportedly shot four times) survived but spent days in the intensive care unit of Grady Memorial Hospital. It was within hours of emergency surgery that English identified Imam Jamil from a photo lineup as the assailant.

In one of the 911 calls that came in that fateful night, the caller identified the sound of persons running, followed by the sound of gunfire. The caller also reported that one of the officers pleaded not to be shot again…but it sounded like he was being shot anyway, as if the assailant was in a rage. On March 17th the Atlanta Journal Constitution would quote David Chadd, public information officer for the Sheriff's Department as follows, "It looked like the gunman had a vendetta for police officers…" And then we have the question of the blood. Was fresh blood found at the scene (as earlier reported)? And if so, whose blood was it?

Surely Allah (God Almighty) knows what really happened the night of March 16th, and who all was involved. We can only speculate. It became clear early on, however, that the official account surrounding this troubling case was seriously flawed from the very beginning. It also appears that persons in high places deliberately determined to make the water even murkier. The question is why?

Deputy English described the eyes of his assailant as gray; and the earliest reports had the assailant wearing a black outer garment – variously described in the earliest reports as a black trench coat, or as a black Islamic style robe. Included in the documentation that we acquired is a "Fulton County Sheriff's Department Incident Report Form." Two things are striking about this document, which comprises a typewritten first-person narration of the March 16th incident given by Deputy English.

First, it's dated May 3, 2000 (almost two months after the incident); secondly, in addition to describing Imam Jamil as having "gray eyes," he also has him wearing (on the night of the tragedy), "a small tan hat, a yellowish cloth quarter length trench coat," and "sunglasses with yellowish lenses."

The "Vagaries" of Eyewitness Identification

> *"The vagaries of eyewitness identification are well known; the annals of criminal law are rife with instances of mistaken identification." – Justice William Brenan*

The state's most potent weapon for conviction was the emotionally delivered eyewitness identification of its star witness, the surviving Sheriff's Deputy Aldranon English. In the words of defense counsel Tony Axum, in closing arguments, "Take away Alabama (where the crux of the circumstantial evidence is) and the prosecution's entire case rests on one man – Deputy English."

Deputy English reportedly identified Imam Jamil from a photo lineup at about 8 am in the morning, after receiving four milligrams of morphine. As stated earlier, English also reported seeing several people around his bed in the hospital who were never there, suggesting he was in a hallucinatory state. How reliable can the identification of a suspect be under such traumatic conditions?

In 1902, Professor von Liszt conducted an experiment in Berlin Germany widely considered to be a landmark study in the psychology of eyewitness testimony. Out of a large seminar class of male students, the one with the best recollection of the staged classroom drama made errors on an estimated 26 percent of the significant details. As a German American scholar at Harvard University, Hugo Munsterberg, would later write: *Words were put into the mouths of men who had been silent spectators during the whole short episode; actions were attributed to the chief participants of which not the slightest trace*

*existed; and essential parts of the tragi-comedy were completely
eliminated from the memory of a number of witnesses."*

Then there is another more recent experiment in the realm of
human psychology that is even more compelling. On December 19,
1974, a short documentary film was shown on a NBC affiliate in New
York. As described in the book entitled Actual Innocence, co-authored
by Barry Scheck, Peter Neufeld, and Jim Dwyer (pg.43):

"A young woman walks in a hallway. A man lurks in a doorway
wearing a hat, leather jacket, and sneakers. The man bursts from the
doorway, grabs the woman's handbag, and runs straight toward the
camera, full faced. The incident lasts twelve seconds. After the film
was shown, the show presented a lineup of suspects. The viewers were
provided with a phone number and asked to choose the culprit from
among those six, or to say that he wasn't in the lineup. "We were
swamped with calls," Robert Buckhout, a professor at Brooklyn
College, who organized the experiment, would later write. "They
unplugged the phone after receiving 2,145 calls."

As it turns out the actual thief (who was in the lineup in position
number two) received a grand total of 302 votes, or 14.1 percent of the
total votes cast. Professor Buckhout would later write an article with
the following headline: *"Nearly 2000 Witnesses Can Be Wrong."*
What is even more significant is when Buckhout used the same purse-
snatching documentary with panels of lawyers and judges, he reported
similar inaccuracy!

"Unconscious Transference"

Elizabeth Loftus, one of the leading researchers in this field of
study, illustrated the phenomenon of unconscious transference, in
which the mind drafts a vaguely familiar face to play a role that could
not otherwise be cast. She extracted a case from real life to illustrate
how this works. A railroad ticket agent who had been robbed at
gunpoint ended up identifying a sailor as his assailant. On the day of
the robbery, however, the sailor had been away at sea. To the

psychologists who reviewed this case, the sailor had been an obvious victim of the unconscious transference phenomenon. He was the one picked out from the lineup, because his face was the most familiar one to the ticket agent. As it turns out, the sailor was based near the railroad station, and had purchased tickets from that very agent three times before the robbery.

On the night of March 16, 2000, deputies Kinchen and English were on the West End to serve a warrant for the arrest of Jamil A. Al-Amin – the same man who was wrongfully charged for a crime he did not commit, and paraded handcuffed and shackled before media cameras five years earlier. When Deputy Aldranon English identified a photograph of Imam Jamil as his assailant (in what defense counsel has labeled a "contaminated" lineup) – within hours of the tragedy, under heavy sedation, and while still in the intensive care unit of Grady Memorial Hospital – is it possible that his identification fit the profile of "unconscious transference?" Only Allah knows. What we do know is that the so-called "facts" which attended the indictment simply did not add up!

In addition to questionable "facts," we also have the reputation of police agencies themselves (federal, state and local). The Human rights Watch report for the year 2000 *("Shielded from Justice: Police Brutality and Accountability in the United States")* examined common obstacles to accountability for police abuse in fourteen large cities, including Atlanta, and concluded: "Police brutality [and other forms of misconduct] is persistent in all of these cities." As for the feds, former Atlanta Mayor Bill Campbell opined in the course of a radio interview in his city, it is a well-known fact among many African Americans that "the FBI has never been a friend of the black community."

> *O you who believe! If a wicked person [or agents of a disreputable government entity] comes to you with any news, ascertain the truth, or you may harm an innocent person unknowingly, and afterwards become full of regret for what you have done. – The Noble Qur'an*

Lastly, we also have what might be described as the Mark Furhman factor injected into this case, in the form of an FBI agent by the name of Ronald Campbell. This factor, coupled with the undeniable fact that Imam Jamil Abdullah Al-Amin did not enjoy his constitutionally guaranteed due process rights to a presumption of innocence, underscored the undeniable, deep rooted political nature of this case.

The FBI Agent Ronald Campbell Factor

FBI Special Agent Ronald Campbell is the "law enforcement officer" who reportedly ran up and kicked Imam Jamil, then spit on him, as he lay handcuffed on the ground on the night of his arrest. By Campbell's own admission he had to be restrained by fellow officers. He is also the agent who fell significantly behind during the chase and is widely suspected of having planted the guns that were later found in the wooded area from which Imam Jamil was said to have emerged.

Special Agent Campbell also holds a special distinction for many residents of the Philadelphia (PA) area; because of an incident that took place on June 1, 1995, when Campbell reportedly shot an unarmed young black man by the name of Glen "Jahlil" Thomas, 23, in the back of the head in broad daylight. The official police version of that incident was called into question after the coroner's report confirmed the street testimony of eyewitnesses; that Thomas had indeed been shot in the back of the head. Later that same year, as a result of mounting protests and community pressure, Campbell was transferred from Philadelphia to the Atlanta division of the FBI.

Mr. Campbell became an active member of the Bureau on September 6, 1988, after completing his training at the FBI Academy, Quantico, Virginia. He was assigned to the Philadelphia division in December of that year. At the time of the West End tragedy he was assigned to the Atlanta Division Special Operations Group, Squad #4, supervised by SSA Robert Kelly, where he performed surveillance activities. He had also been a member of the Atlanta Division Special Weapons and Tactics (SWAT) Team since about February 1996.

Campbell and the team to which he was assigned arrived in the White Hall area on Saturday morning, March 18, to begin their surveillance operation. On Monday (March 20th) he wore his FBI SWAT soft body armor vest, blue jeans, an ear plug for his Bureau radio attached to his body armor, his Bureau issued weapon in his SWAT holster, and an ankle holster with a Bureau approved weapon. He was also armed with a M-4 long gun. (This is important to note, given the claim of no gunfire from law enforcement on the night of Imam Jamil's arrest.)

In a sworn affidavit Campbell describes the scene on the night of the arrest; the plane, the dogs, the helicopter, accompanied by a horde of cops from different agencies. He also describes in detail how he fell behind during the chase, and how he felt embarrassed and became upset with himself. After Imam Jamil's apprehension he describes the scene and touches upon what he did: "I see a big crowd of law enforcement officers.

I approach this group and see Al-Amin handcuffed, with his hands behind his back, laying on the ground, on his side. My spider sense turned on, this is the guy that shot at us (me). I kicked him in his upper leg or buttocks. My kick was not a gentle nudge but was intended more to get his attention than to inflict injury. He looked up at me and I said, This is what we do to cop killers. Al-Amin looked at me when I kicked him, he said something that provoked me. I don't specifically recall what he said, but its meaning was fuck you. I spit at him but didn't hit him… Someone grabbed the back of my armor vest at the collar and tugged me back saying something to the effect 'easy' or 'Ron.'"

Clearly, Agent Campbell was out of control. This was Monday, March 20, 2000. By his admission, Campbell didn't discuss the incident with anyone between the time of Imam Jamil's arrest and July 2001! He also admits in the affidavit that he did not include mention of this incident in his official report(s), although he was cautioned, "The incident did not go unnoticed." He states in the affidavit:

The OPR Interviewers have told me that a local law enforcement officer has allegedly remarked that, based upon activity observed at the arrest scene, Al-Amin's life might have been in danger had officers from his department not been present at the arrest scene." (This writer agrees with that conclusion.)

This is the same Agent Ronald Campbell who shot 23 year old Glen "Jahlil" Thomas in the back of the head in broad daylight five years earlier; the same Agent Campbell who - along with other "officers of the law" who provided cover - lied about that unwarranted police homicide. The same Agent Campbell who fell behind in the chase in Lowndes County, Alabama; and the same Agent Campbell who many believe was capable of planting weapons in a wooded area in order to get his man. (ALLAH knows best)

CHAPTER 4 - The Aftermath

This chapter examines the aftermath of a deeply flawed trial, and the beginning of a new phase of struggle. In it we get a glimpse into the interwoven links of how the system works – both state and federal – in producing what we in the human rights community call "a political prisoner."

The Cold Fingers of the State Get Their Man

Of special note is the following: Imam Jamil was originally scheduled to stand trial in federal court in Montgomery, Alabama, on Monday, December 9, 2002, for allegedly firing a weapon at federal officers on the night of his arrest. Days before the trial was set to begin, US District Court Judge Charles S. Coody dismissed the case "without prejudice" - meaning the government could bring it back before another judge at a later date if he or she chose to do so. Truth be told, the government may have had second thoughts about a federal prosecution for ulterior motives.

During the state trial testimony was given by residents of White Hall, Alabama, that contradicted the government's claim that Imam Jamil fired a weapon during the chase, and law enforcement officers did not. (Notable also is the fact that there was *no gunshot residue* found on Imam Jamil's person after he was taken into custody.)

The award-winning journalist and internationally renowned U.S. political prisoner Mumia Abu-Jamal, gave the following cautionary note before the start of the Georgia State trial: *"The struggle for the freedom and liberty of Atlanta Muslim leader Imam Jamil Abdullah Al-Amin must take place now, before the cold fingers of the state can close around his neck. Al-Amin's freedom lies in people who express their support now, instead of later. Fairness does not lie in reversing an unjust conviction; rather it lies in preventing one in the first place."*

How prophetic his words. Unfortunately, we collectively failed to pay heed to this insightful warning, and that failure brought us to where we are today. After three weeks of testimony and argumentation, followed by ten hours of deliberation, the jury convicted Imam Jamil on all 13 counts in the indictment. After five additional hours of deliberation for the penalty phase, the jury decided on a sentence of life imprisonment without the possibility of parole.

While the State got its conviction - via what many consider to be a severely tainted process - it fell short of its ultimate goal (the death penalty). Many believe former US Ambassador Andrew Young's character witness testimony, during the sentencing phase of the trial, was a critical factor in the outcome (life imprisonment instead of a death sentence). The establishment was in full celebratory mode nevertheless. The day after the sentencing (3/13/02) an editorial appeared in the *Atlanta Journal-Constitution* newspaper that read: **"Al-Amin will die in prison, obscure and long forgotten."**

The response of Imam Jamil's supporters has been: Time is the best tester of men and ideas; that declaration will not go unchallenged! If the proceedings had been fair and transparent in the fullest sense of the word, with the "facts" at the end of the day pointing undeniably to Imam Jamil's guilt, it would be easier to accept the outcome. Muslims would be forced to draw lessons from a good and committed life gone awry. However, with the process being as it was, and the outcome coming as it did, committed Muslims and non-Muslim supporters were left with one option – to struggle on.

As Mrs. Coretta Scott King so eloquently stated when the trial commenced, *"This tragedy must not be compounded by a flawed trial or a rushed verdict… If these standards are scrupulously observed and reflected in the outcome, then the healing process can begin."*

It has now been 20 years, but the "healing process" has yet to begin!

The Ghosts of COINTELPRO

"Each man is three men: the one he thinks he is; the one others think he is; and the one he really is." - Wordsworth

The gatekeepers of the state have one image of the man formerly known as H. Rap Brown; but theirs is not the only image. When this writer posed a question to former U.S. Attorney General Ramsey Clark in a press conference at the National Press Club in Washington, DC (not long after the trial had ended in 2002), Clark's response was immediate and straight to the point: "Let me say first, I remember Rap Brown well from the 60s, and I thought that he was a splendid human being and leader of the civil rights movement…with a strong touch of nobility and commitment. I remember when Congress passed the H. Rap Brown law, just to try to get people like him; and finally, he was indicted under the law that he honored with his name."

The aforementioned response from a man who once occupied the highest law enforcement office in the land reflects another image of this controversial figure. As Professor Clark and I departed the press conference that day engaged in [looking back on history] conversation, he had more to say about the man who evolved into the personality known today as Imam Jamil Abdullah Al-Amin. Comments that would echo the second part of his response to the question I raised earlier at the press conference - regarding connections between the case of Imam Jamil, the so-called "war on terrorism," and mounting civil liberties concerns in the USA.

Clark stated:

There can be no question that the United States government – through its intelligence agencies and most of its appointed leadership, and a great deal of its elected leadership – considers Islam, not just militant Islam, but Islam, to be the greatest threat to the domestic and international security of the United States.

While many within the establishment make the argument that *"everything changed after 9/11"* - this writer has argued for years that the war on Islam and Muslims preceded the controversial attacks of September 11, 2001. I am not alone in this opinion. The late Bill Kunstler has a chapter in his thought-provoking book (<u>My Life As A Radical Lawyer</u>, published by Carol Publishing Group, 1994) that supports this argument as well. The chapter is titled *"The Despised Muslim."* On its opening page there is a paragraph that reads: "Today Muslims are the most hated group in the country; the moment a Muslim is accused of a crime, the specter of terrorism is raised, and everyone panics." With this in mind it's easy to see how for some operating within the shadows of what's euphemistically called "The Deep State," H. Rap Brown never left the "Most Wanted" public enemy roster.

During the "discovery" process leading up to the trial, we learned that Imam Jamil and the West End Community Mosque was the target of a five-year undercover investigation, conducted by a special task force comprised of local and federal officers. This "probe" allegedly lasted from 1992-1997 and included paid informants (and probably agent-provocateurs) planted within The Community Mosque. On August 7, 1995, Imam Jamil was arrested and paraded before the media for allegedly shooting a young man in the leg. The effort to implicate Imam Jamil backfired when the young man publicly disclosed that he had told the authorities he did not know who shot him; and further, that he was pressured into saying it was Imam Jamil. The day following his arrest Imam Jamil was released on bail, and charges were never pursued. Needless to say, this brought a number of well-informed observers in the activist community to certain well founded conclusions.

COINTELPRO was the Federal Bureau of Investigation's COunter INTELligence PROgram, established under the late J. Edgar Hoover. It began in the 1950s as a response to Communism. It was later expanded to target and attack certain African American leaders and organizations, and anyone else who Director Hoover and his associates considered a "threat to America's national security." The targets were varied, from "civil rights" icons like the Rev. Dr. Martin Luther King, Jr. and the Southern Christian Leadership Conference, to human rights/black power advocates like Malcolm X, Stokely Carmichael, H. Rap Brown, and the Black Panther Party. Sound familiar?

In a [then] classified memo dated August 25, 1967, the objectives for the further expansion of COINTELPRO were graphically laid out:

> *The purpose of this new counterintelligence endeavor is to expose, disrupt, misdirect, or otherwise neutralize the activities of black nationalist, hate-type organizations and groupings, their leadership, spokesmen, membership and supporters, and to counter their propensity for violence and civil disorder...*

Another passage reads:

No opportunity should be missed to exploit through counterintelligence techniques the organizational and personal conflicts of the leaderships of the [targeted] groups, and where possible an effort should be made to capitalize upon existing conflicts between competing black nationalist organizations. When an opportunity is apparent to disrupt or neutralize black nationalist, hate type organizations through cooperation of established local news media contacts, or through such contact with sources available to the seat of government, in every instance careful attention must be given to that proposal to insure the targeted group is disrupted and not merely publicized. Consideration should be given to techniques to preclude violence-prone or rabble rouser leaders of hate groups from spreading their philosophy publicly, or through various mass communication media.

The COINTELPRO memo also read:

*Intensified attention under this program should be afforded to activities of such groups as the Student Nonviolent Coordinating Committee, the Southern Christian Leadership Conference, Revolutionary Action Movement, the Deacons for Defense and Justice, Congress of Racial Equality, and the Nation of Islam. Particular emphasis should be given to extremists who direct the activities and polices of revolutionary or militant groups, such as Stokely Carmichael, **H. "Rap" Brown**, Elijah Muhammad, and Maxwell Stanford.*

It should be noted here that the Southern Christian Leadership Conference (SCLC) was an organization founded and led by Rev. Dr. Martin Luther King Jr. It was an organization predicated on direct action for social change through the prism of creative non-violence, reinforced by the moral principle of forgiveness and atonement; and yet this organization and its leaders (particularly, Dr. King) were vigorously targeted. If one were to transpose "black nationalist" with 'Muslim' we would be compelled to acknowledge the fact that

COINTELPRO on steroids is still being employed today; and further, that today's targets are just as philosophically diverse as they were in the 60s.

If there is one undeniable truth that life has taught me, it is the fact that life is cyclical. Names and faces change, but the pattern of human behavior remains the same. COINTELPRO Lives!

From State to Federal

We in America often boast of how the Unites States' system of jurisprudence is head and shoulders above all others around the world. This not my view, and surely Allah (God Almighty) knows best. One thing is clear; much too often our adversarial system of "justice" has shown itself to be not so much about uncovering facts, discovering truth, and establishing justice; but merely winning. Winning (by any means necessary) is everything! This is a negative paradigm that people of conscience should seek to reform. The long-term health and welfare of the better of the two Americas depends on it.

Despite troubling questions and inconsistencies in the state's case – i.e., the wounded assailant and blood controversy; the assailant's grey eyes; the ever changing description of the assailant's attire; the bleeding mystery man begging for a ride; the Otis Jackson confessions; the Agent Campbell factor; and finally, the lack of hard evidence – Imam Jamil was nevertheless convicted of all 13 counts in the Superior Court of Fulton County, Georgia, and given a sentence of life without the possibility of parole.

After the trial ended, Imam Jamil was taken to Jackson for diagnostics testing under tight security. During the flight he was reportedly adorned with an electronic sleeve that carried 50,000 volts of electricity, in addition to being handcuffed in a very uncomfortable position. After his diagnostics was complete, he was transferred to the maximum-security prison in Reidsville, Georgia – a town located midway between Macon and Savannah, about a three-hour drive from Atlanta. At Reidsville, depending upon who you talk to, Imam Jamil was placed in "protective custody" under a high level of security for: (a) "his own safety," or (b) because he was considered a "security threat to the institution." He was handcuffed and/or shackled whenever he was moved within the institution (even when he showered), and he was kept in his cell 23 hours of each day, permitted one hour of "recreation" inside and outdoor cage.

Needless to say, he was not permitted to properly observe a religious obligation he has as a practicing Muslim (i.e., the congregational jumah prayer service). Despite these onerous restrictions, however, he was still able to share the message of Islam (give *dawah*) and reportedly presided over a number of shahadahs (conversions) within the prison. One in particular is of special note. A former leader of the Aryan Brotherhood - a violent white supremacist group at the Reidsville State Prison - who was once known as "Jelly Roll," embraced Islam and became known by the beautiful name: Abdullah Nasr. Imam Jamil also received messages of solidarity from the inmate population at the prison – which [then] housed about 2,000 men, about 300 of whom were reportedly Caucasian. The messages of solidarity came from black and white inmates.

Despite this highly restrictive custody arrangement, Imam Jamil was treated early on with unusual deference by the administration. When he first arrived he was visited in his cell by the warden of the institution, who wanted to explain certain things about his custody arrangement and to note that if the Imam experienced anything that he felt was abusive or uncalled for, he could bring this to the immediate attention of the warden, rather than lodge a complaint through his attorney. For example, the authorities wanted Sr. Karima to remove her hijab (Islamic head covering) when she came to visit her husband. This, needless to say, had to be quickly resolved.

A guard was reportedly killed at Reidsville about 24 years earlier, and this, no doubt, coupled with all of the hype about this "former Black Panther" and "convicted cop killer," is what initially had some of the prison personnel on edge. The irony was that Imam Jamil could have been one of the most positive stabilizing forces within the entire institution; and a contributor to a process of genuine inmate "rehabilitation" - had he not been transferred into federal custody and imprisoned in America's only "supermax" facility in Florence, Colorado, where he spent years of abusive solitary confinement!

Post-Conviction Appeals Process

At the time of this writing it's been 18 years since the trial that put Imam Jamil Abdullah Al-Amin behind bars under a life sentence, with the appeals process taking many twists and turns. For the sake of time and clarity we will focus solely on the latest chapter of this ongoing saga.

On May 3, 2019, supporters of Imam Jamil from across the country (Muslim and non-Muslim), packed a courtroom in downtown Atlanta, where a three-judge panel of the *11th U.S. Circuit Court of Appeals* heard arguments in the constitutional challenge to his ongoing imprisonment and request for a new trial. Among the issues at hand were the following:

- during closing arguments, the lead prosecutor violated the imam's constitutional right not to testify, by making a prejudicial argument against his decision to observe his fifth amendment privilege;
- the imam's lawyers were denied the opportunity to question Agent Campbell, a federal law enforcement officer with a troubling history, and troubling behavior on the night of Imam Jamil's arrest;
- the omission from the trial of Otis Jackson, a man who confessed to being the assailant who shot the sheriff deputies on March 16, 2000;
- the controversy that still surrounds the blood trail that led to an abandoned house around the corner from the scene of the crime, coupled with the earlier assertion that the assailant had been shot. (When Imam Jamil was taken into custody days later, he had no injuries.)

The judges grilled both sides during the hearing. Circuit Judge Charles Wilson seemed especially troubled by the prosecutor's conduct, repeatedly calling it egregious. But he also said the physical evidence from Alabama and English's in-court identification of Al-Amin was difficult to overcome. At the end of the day, most of the observers present (this writer included) felt that the arguments were strongly in Imam Jamil's favor. We left the courthouse that day feeling optimistic that a new trial was inevitable; and that if a new trial was held, with all of the evidence allowed to come in, a full exoneration was also inevitable. After two months passed, and a decision had still not been rendered by the court, supporters of the imam decided to convey a message of communal concern.

On Friday, July 26, 2019, supporters of Imam Jamil (once again from different parts of the country) converged in front of the CNN Center in downtown Atlanta for a support rally. The demonstration was meant to send a message to the 11th Circuit Court of Appeals that Imam Jamil's supporters were still waiting for the decision of the court and would not allow their concern for him to wane. Five days later on July 31st a decision was rendered. Once again, Imam Jamil was <u>denied</u> a new trial.

Is Justice Possible for a Political Prisoner?

Before revisiting the 11th Circuit's decision, let us briefly revisit an earlier appeals decision in another court. In September 2017, U.S. District Court Judge Amy Totenberg found that Al-Amin's constitutional right not to testify *was* violated by the prosecutor's questioning. She also found that the trial court's attempt to mitigate the prosecutor's violation was insufficient and may have actually been harmful. However, "there is weighty evidence supporting his conviction," she wrote.

Lawyers for Al-Amin countered that there is even stronger evidence pointing to his innocence. Totenberg conceded that the evidence presented a "mishmash of inconsistencies," but that evidence recovered in Alabama when he was arrested "strongly ties" him to the crime. Another reminder of how the presumption of innocence principle only applies to certain types of "criminals." Here I am reminded of an observation made by the late New York State Supreme Court Justice Bruce Wright, who said: *"Racism in the courts is camouflaged by politeness. Racism is camouflaged by judges not saying, 'Nigger, I'm going to give you the maximum.' Racism is camouflaged by judges acting as though everything is OK, everything is equal, but making up their minds in advance..."* (Source: <u>Black Judges On Justice</u>, Linn Washington, pg. 247)

Al-Amin's lawyers also argued that the court violated his rights by refusing to allow his lawyers to cross-examine one of the FBI agents involved in his arrest about an earlier incident in which the agent was accused of shooting an unarmed black man in Philadelphia, and putting a gun with no fingerprints on it next to the man's body. The guns used to shoot the Georgia deputies that were allegedly found in the vicinity of Al-Amin's arrest in Alabama also had no prints, and his lawyers contend that the same agent planted them. The trial court excluded that evidence because the agent had been "investigated and cleared" in the Philadelphia incident. Totenberg said the trial court was within its rights to make that decision.

Overall, Totenberg found there wasn't "sufficient cumulative error" to find his imprisonment unconstitutional. While the violation of his right not to testify was "serious and repeated," Totenberg said she was constrained by the "onerous standards" imposed by the law and Supreme Court case law. Judge Totenberg ruled in the State's favor. Imam Jamil Abdullah Al-Amin's attorneys wanted the United States Court of Appeals for the Eleventh Circuit to reverse the lower court's ruling.

Thoughts on the 11th Circuit's Decision

Back in the day when I was a young man coming up in the organization known as The Nation of Islam, we used to have a term called "tricknology." This term came to mind after I read the following lines on pages 10 & 11 of the court's decision: "When a defendant alleges a non-structural constitutional error at his trial, a state court reviewing a conviction on direct review analyzes the error under the standard established in Chapman v. California. (1967 case law.) Under the Chapman standard, 'A constitutional violation is harmless if the government can show beyond a reasonable doubt that the error did not contribute to the verdict."

The jurists in this case than take it a step further stating (on page 10): "But on collateral review, we apply a more stringent harmless error standard. Under *Brecht* [referring to *Brecht v. Abrahamson*,1993 case law] we cannot grant habeas relief unless we have 'grave doubt' that the constitutional error 'had substantial and injurious effect or influence in determining the jury's verdict." (And here they cited another piece of case law, from 1995, known as *O'neal v. McAninch*, which supposedly explains the *Brecht* standard.) "To prevail, a petitioner must show 'actual prejudice' from constitutional error… To show prejudice under Brecht, there must be more than a reasonable possibility that the error contributed to the conviction or sentence."

The jurists then state: "Harmlessness under the *Brecht* standard is a question of law that we review de novo. Ultimately, for a federal court to grant habeas relief, it must be true <u>both</u> that the state court's application of the Chapman harmless beyond a reasonable doubt standard was objectively unreasonable, and that the error had a substantial and injurious effect or influence on the verdict."

(*This term *de novo* is quite interesting; the essential meaning is to begin anew. In law, it signifies beginning a new trial, by a different tribunal – which is precisely what Imam Jamil and his legal team were trying to accomplish!)

Now in my humble opinion, there is no question that Imam Jamil's Fifth and Fourteenth Amendment rights were violated during his trial – when the lead prosecutor engaged in that mock cross-examination during closing arguments. There is also no doubt in my mind that the imam's Sixth and Fourteenth Amendment rights were further violated when the defense was prevented from cross examining FBI Agent Ron Campbell about the circumstances surrounding his past fatal shooting of an unarmed black man in Philadelphia.

When the appeals court published their decision five days after a citizens rally for Imam Jamil in the city of Atlanta, home of the 11th Circuit Court of Appeals, denying this political prisoner judicial relief in his quest for a new trial – was it coincidence? Perhaps. ALLAH knows best. What I know for a fact is that if the powers that be expected that decision to quell the activism around this political prisoner's plight, they are in for a rude awakening.

CHAPTER 5 - Other Voices

In the pages of this chapter we hear from a number of voices who weigh in on the life, legacy, and ongoing struggle of Imam Jamil Abdullah Al-Amin. We begin with a thought-provoking article penned by Obaid H. Siddiqui, a writer and freelance journalist based in Philadelphia. (The article first appeared in TheRoot.com on 5/30/18)

Obaid H. Siddiqui: The Unofficial Gag Order of Jamil Al-Amin

Obaid H. Siddiqui is a freelance writer and journalist based in Philadelphia. He is a contributor to the anthology "All-American: 45 American Men on Being Muslim." He can be followed on Twitter @OhSiddiqui.

At the modern intersection of Islamophobia and the Black Lives Matter movement resides Jamil Al-Amin (formerly H. Rap Brown), the now forgotten civil rights activist and revolutionary leader who, 16 years ago this year, was sentenced to life imprisonment for the murder of Fulton County, Ga., Sheriff's Deputy Ricky Leon Kinchen and the wounding of his partner, then-Sheriff's Deputy Aldranon English, during a March 2000 gunfight.

On the night of March 16, 2000, Deputies Kinchen and English were serving a warrant for the arrest of Al-Amin for missing a court hearing regarding a traffic stop when they were engaged in a gun battle outside Al-Amin's grocery store in the West End neighborhood of Atlanta. Kinchen died the next day in the hospital, and English, who had wounds that reminded arriving paramedic Kristin McGregor Jones of "Vietnam War wounds that I've seen in the movies," later identified Al-Amin as the shooter before being rushed into surgery.

Prior to his murder trial, Al-Amin released a statement proclaiming his innocence and empathy for the family of Kinchen. Afterward, the trial judge, Stephanie B. Manis, placed a gag order on Al-Amin to prevent him from speaking. That gag order has unofficially been reinstated over the past 10 years, ever since Al-Amin was secretly moved from a state prison in Georgia to the federal Administrative-Maximum (ADX) supermax prison in Florence, Colo., amounting to the de facto silencing of a man who has been targeted by the federal government for decades and who many believe is innocent of the crimes for which he's been convicted.

A Perceived Threat

Multiple writers, journalists, filmmakers and academics have attempted to reach out through the federal Bureau of Prisons to interview Al-Amin. All requests have been denied or ignored.

Early in 2017, professor and author Arun Kundnani, who is currently working on a biography of Al-Amin, "initiated the process [and] went through the paperwork," but was told that an interview of Al-Amin would not be allowed to take place. *"Every scholar and journalist has been denied over the past 10 years because of a 'security risk,'" Kundnani said.*

The apparent "security risk" posed by Al-Amin stems from his time in the Georgia State Prison at Reidsville, where he was first imprisoned to serve his life sentence. Through the prison mail system, Al-Amin was asked to represent the needs of Muslim prisoners in the Georgia prison system. Yusha Abdul-Quddos, a prisoner at Reidsville at the time, asked Al-Amin to *"facilitate and encourage communication between Muslim inmates and the Reidsville prison administration,"* according to Al-Amin when he explained the intent of the communication to prison authorities.

Al-Amin accepted, later explaining to prison officials that he wanted to *"help Muslim inmates achieve the same religious privileges afforded to inmates of other religions."* An intelligence unit within the prison inferred a greater threat and, after investigating the situation, released three reports that ultimately acknowledged that Al-Amin never *"ordered other inmates at any prison to commit violence against prison officials"* and was not tied, directly or indirectly, to any violence or unrest. Still, the unit requested that Al-Amin step down from his leadership role, and he acquiesced.

Two months later, though, on June 12, 2006, the FBI prepared a report based on the information gathered from the prison intelligence unit titled, "The Attempt to Radicalize the Georgia Department of Corrections' Inmate Muslim Population." The purpose of the FBI report was to *"provide insight into the motivation of a radical extremist exploiting an inmate population for personal gain and power."* Identifying Al-Amin as the "radical extremist," the report went on to state, *"The solidarity movement could unify radical extremists, resulting in a power base within the inmate population which could promote organized recruitment drives for radical Islamist and collective disruptive or subversive behavior."*

The report claimed that the "assertion that one of the missions of the movement is to promote and defend the interests of incarcerated Muslims" was one of many "security and radicalization concerns."

The Prison Shuffle

On July 30, 2007, a year after the FBI report, which lacked a single bit of evidence tying Al-Amin to extremism, Al-Amin was secretly transferred to the federal ADX prison without the knowledge of his family or legal counsel.

Al-Amin spent seven years in solitary confinement in the ADX, where he was locked in an underground cell for 23 hours a day. By early 2013, he'd developed a **dental abscess** that, by October 2013, had caused his jaw to swell. "He had fluid gushing out of his mouth [and began] swallowing the toxic fluids," said Karima Al-Amin, Al-Amin's wife and lawyer. When she spoke with him in 2014, he sounded as if he was "out of breath, as if he was running; he had difficulty breathing," Karima Al-Amin said. *The toxic fluids "had gone into his lungs and chest area."*

While Al-Amin languished in the ADX with an increasingly serious medical condition, thousands of miles from his home in Atlanta, his family became worried. It was "rough for us, realizing he's up in age now, thinking he's in a cell and can't get proper medical attention," said Karima Al-Amin. The situation is "so emotionally draining. It finally hit Kairi [one of their sons] when he couldn't sleep. Just thinking about his father's health made Kairi break down." After his wife led a campaign to get her husband proper medical attention, Al-Amin was moved to the Butner Federal Medical Center, a federal prison in North Carolina, in July 2014.

Having formally been treated for the abscess, Al-Amin was then moved to the U.S. Penitentiary, Canaan, a federal prison in Pennsylvania. For the first time in his life sentence imprisonment, Al-Amin was placed in general population, out of solitary confinement. But by early 2016 he was moved again, this time to U.S. Penitentiary, Tucson, a federal prison in Arizona, where he is currently held, cut off from speaking to the outside world.

An Open Letter to the Federal Bureau of Prisons

Through "policy documents made available by the Georgia Department of Corrections, the BOP [Bureau of Prisons] ... assessed that [Al-Amin] is a security risk—someone who is convicted of harming a law enforcement officer is a certain risk," said Kundnani, who is seeking to interview Al-Amin in the Arizona prison. "But while at Reidsville, he was granted interviews," Kundnani pointed out. Therefore, "the reason they give now—nature of conviction—would have applied earlier, not just over the past 10 years."

"Serial killers are interviewed in prison, but he's not allowed to communicate with the outside world in the form of an interview. It's something that needs to be addressed," Kundnani said.

As a result, Kundnani published an open letter in December 2017 aimed at the BOP and the state of Georgia, demanding an end to the isolation of Al-Amin and allowing academics and journalists access to him. Kundnani hopes that the open letter can get enough support from the world of academia so that he can "go back to the BOP and ask them to review their decision in unjustly silencing [Al-Amin]."

"The suggestion that I'd be in danger by interviewing him, that's ridiculous. Whose security is at risk?" Kundnani asked rhetorically. "So the reason must lie somewhere else."

A Decades long Target

Federal authorities have long sought to discredit, silence and punish Al-Amin. As part of the FBI's illegal Counterintelligence Program, or COINTELPRO, J. Edgar Hoover sent a memorandum dated Aug. 25, 1967, to all FBI offices regarding "Black Nationalist Hate Groups" (eerily similar to the supposed current "black identity extremist" threat identified by the FBI).

The memo ordered all FBI offices to "expose, disrupt, misdirect, discredit, or otherwise neutralize" all individuals and organizations considered a threat. Al-Amin, then H. Rap Brown, listed among three others—Stokely Carmichael (Kwame Ture), Elijah Muhammad and Maxwell Stanford (Muhammad Ahmed)—was to be given "particular emphasis."

The surveillance continued throughout the 1990s, as the FBI placed informants in Al-Amin's Atlanta community to try to connect him with criminal activity. Despite developing a 44,000-page file on Al-Amin, the FBI was unable to pin a single charge on him. That all changed in May of 1999, when Al-Amin was pulled over by Cobb County, Ga., Police Officer Johnny Mack for driving a vehicle with a "drive-out tag," which legally allowed new car owners to drive a vehicle for 30 days without officially registering it.

In a court hearing, Mack explained that stopping cars with drive-out tags was part of his "basic patrol," even when there was no evidence of wrongdoing. In light of new documents that were released by the FBI in 2013 per a long-standing Freedom of Information Act request initiated by Al-Amin's wife, however, the traffic stop appears more targeted than random. On April 14, 1999, six weeks before Mack pulled over Al-Amin on May 31, an FBI document logging surveillance on Al-Amin stated he was "observed unloading unidentified items from a dark green Ford Explorer with dealer tags."

According to Mack's testimony, he ran a check on the vehicle identification number and the car was listed as stolen. At that point, Al-Amin was removed from his vehicle and searched. During the pat-down, Mack found a bill of sale for the vehicle and a police badge in Al-Amin's wallet. The bill of sale showed Al-Amin as the rightful owner of the vehicle and that the honorary badge had been issued to Al-Amin from the former mayor of White Hall, Ala., John Jackson.

Al-Amin never presented the badge, and following the arrest, the mayor of White Hall sent a letter to officials in Georgia verifying the authenticity of the honorary badge. Still, Al-Amin was charged with driving a stolen car, driving with expired insurance and impersonating a police officer. After missing the court date for the traffic hearing, which Al-Amin asserts he was never told of after it had been rescheduled following a severe ice storm that hit Atlanta, Deputies Kinchen and English went to serve the warrant for his arrest that led to the gunfight.

Disputed Evidence

Al-Amin's trial lasted two months [from the start of jury selection to the verdict]. Multiple elements of the prosecution's narrative didn't fit the physical evidence of the crime scene. The surviving deputy, English, swore that his attacker had gray eyes and that he and Kinchen had shot him. There were multiple 911 calls made after the shooting that identified a man "bleeding on the corner begging for a ride." But Al-Amin has brown eyes and, when captured four days after the gunfight, had no signs of any shooting-related injuries.

A witness testified that upon hearing shots fired, he looked out his window and saw a man of "average height, average build" firing a gun and was "absolutely positive" it wasn't Al-Amin, who has a distinctively lean, 6-foot-5-inch frame.

Moreover, the guns found in Alabama during the arrest of Al-Amin did not have any fingerprints on them; nor did Al-Amin have any residue from shooting the guns on his hands or clothes. The latter was an important detail: Federal officers claimed that Al-Amin shot at them during his capture, and they even filed a federal indictment against him. The charges were dismissed in 2002 after multiple witnesses testified that federal officers were the only ones firing their weapons.

In addition, the prosecution provided no motive. No explanation was given as to why a well-respected religious leader of a burgeoning Atlanta community, on the night of one of the holiest days in the Muslim calendar—Eid al-Adha—would shoot at two black deputies serving him a warrant for missing a traffic-stop hearing.

Despite the lack of motive and actual evidence, the jury of nine blacks, two whites and one Hispanic returned a guilty verdict after five hours of deliberation. The jury decided against the death penalty and instead committed Al-Amin to life in prison. The same day that his conviction was delivered, the state trial court ruled that the original traffic stop that started the whole ordeal had violated Al-Amin's Fourth Amendment right of protection from unreasonable search and seizure, and therefore had been illegal.

Since then, Al-Amin has been secretly moved from a state prison in Georgia to federal custody, where, at USP, Tucson, he is currently imprisoned and still actively working with his lawyers to petition for a retrial.

The Appeal

The appeal for a retrial is being led by the law firm Kilpatrick Townsend & Stockton. KT&S originally was assigned Al-Amin's case pro bono when he brought a suit against the warden of the Georgia State Prison, Hugh Smith, and other prison officials for illegally opening mail from his legal counsel in violation of Georgia Department of Corrections' procedures and Al-Amin's constitutional rights. As he researched the case, Allen Garrett and lead counsel and senior partner at KT&S A. Stephens Clay discovered retaliatory actions on the part of prison officials against Al-Amin. Moreover, they came across the work of G. Terry Jackson and Linda Sheffield, Al-Amin's attorneys from his state appeal case in 2007.

The 2007 state appeal featured a deposition of Otis Jackson, a man who, on three separate occasions, confessed to the crime for which Al-Amin is imprisoned. Jackson's deposition provided accurate details of the night of the shooting, from the type of weapons and ammunition used to the position of the deputies and vehicles during the shootout. Jackson also matches the physical description of the eyewitness who saw the shooter—Jackson is listed as 5 feet 8 inches tall and 170 pounds, and he has gray eyes, matching the testimony given by Deputy English of the man who shot him.

Photo: Florida Department of Corrections

Jackson's confession also matches the 911 calls reporting a bleeding man making his way through the neighborhood: In his confession he describes knocking on doors and trying to hitch a ride while bleeding from his wounds. Jackson even has scars on his body from wounds he says were caused by the guns of the deputies during the gunfight. (Jackson, also known as James Santos, is currently serving a prison sentence at U.S. Penitentiary, McCreary, in Kentucky, for unrelated crimes. He is scheduled to be released in 2027.)

On March 7, Al-Amin's current lawyers submitted an appeal petitioning for a new trial with the 11th U.S. Circuit Court of Appeals in Georgia, partly based on ignored evidence contradicting the prosecution's claims, like the multiple confessions of Otis Jackson that were never presented to the jury, and blatant violations of Al-Amin's constitutional rights during the original trial. During the prosecution's closing arguments, a mock cross-examination was performed of Al-

Amin—a gross violation of his Fifth Amendment right not to testify or to have his choice used against him, as the prosecution did.

Planting Guns

Al-Amin's defense was also refused the chance to cross-examine FBI agent Ron Campbell, a violation of the confrontation clause within the Sixth Amendment. Not only did Campbell admit to angrily spitting on and kicking Al-Amin after he was handcuffed, but his story concerning where he was during the hunt for Al-Amin prior to his capture was also inconsistent. At one point, while looking through the wooded area where Al-Amin eventually was arrested, Campbell claimed that he was helped over a fence by other officers. Later, Campbell claimed that he was alone when he climbed the fence.

The details of Campbell's story are important, specifically in relation to the finding of the guns at the scene and when he was alone. Although federal officers claimed that Al-Amin fired weapons at them prior to his arrest—a claim that was later dropped after multiple witnesses contradicted the charge—the guns found at the scene had neither fingerprints, DNA, nor blood tying them to Al-Amin.

Al-Amin's lawyers believe that Campbell planted the guns at the scene, referencing an incident five years earlier in 1995, when Campbell killed Glenn Thomas, a 23-year-old black man in Philadelphia.

Autopsy shows fugitive was shot in back of head

An article in the Philadelphia Inquirer about 23-year-old Glenn Thomas'
death after he was killed by FBI agent Ron Campbell

On June 1, 1995, Campbell and three Philadelphia police officers
approached Thomas while he was sitting on a railing with two friends
drinking a milkshake. Thomas was wanted for skipping bail and
missing a court hearing for charges stemming from an assault on
Housing Authority officers six months earlier. Thomas started to run,
but before he could get far, he was shot and killed by Campbell. The
FBI and the Philadelphia officers claimed that Thomas pulled a gun
and turned toward them to fire. However, witnesses to the shooting
said Thomas didn't have a gun.

Further contradicting Campbell's claim was the fact that Thomas
was shot in the back of the head and the gun found next to him had no
fingerprints on it, leading many to believe the gun was planted on
Thomas by Campbell.

Al-Amin's defense wanted to question Campbell about his history
of being accused of planting weapons on suspects, but the judge
denied the attempt because Campbell, though investigated by the
FBI's Internal Affairs unit and subjected to a private criminal
complaint calling for his arrest in the Superior Court of Pennsylvania,
was never found guilty. Now, 16 years after his conviction and 10
years since any journalist or academic has been able to interview him,
Al-Amin sits in a federal prison, waiting for his case to make its way
through the court of appeals. All the while, his family and supporters
believe he's innocent and simply another targeted victim of a decades-
old federal vendetta.

"We Don't Want You Talking"

The de facto silencing of Al-Amin is "more about what he
represents, not the nature of his conviction. The government believes
he's a radical voice among Muslims and black people, and they'd
rather that his followers did not hear from him," said Kundnani.

Khalil Abdul-Rahman, a close friend of Al-Amin's and a leader of a Muslim community in Greensboro, N.C., recalled seeing Al-Amin in 2013 as a legal assistant to former U.S. Attorney General Ramsey Clark, who visited Al-Amin at the ADX supermax prison in Colorado. Al-Amin was "allowed out in the yard for a little bit with a few other prisoners ... the Hispanic prisoners gravitated toward him, and when they were called back in, they asked the guards for Qurans," Abdul-Rahman said. "The [then] warden [David Berkebile] was watching the whole time," and he turned to Al-Amin and said, "'This is why we don't want you talking.'"

Special note: This article first appeared at theroot.com on 5/30/18

Hamzah Raza: "Potential Retrial in Sight"

Hamzah Raza is a graduate student at Harvard University and an alumnus of Vanderbilt University. At Vanderbilt, he received highest honors for his thesis on the role that South African Muslims played in the anti-apartheid struggle. He has been previously been published at the Huffington Post, Alternet, the Grayzone Project, Raw Story, and the Tennessean. Follow him on Twitter @raza_hamzah (This article first appeared in MuslimMatters.org in May 2019)

It was the night of March 16th, 2000. It was the night before Eid, the holiest day of the year for West End's Muslim community. Prayers would be led by Imam Jamil Al-Amin, the soft-spoken, bookish Imam, who was famously known in the civil rights movement as H. Rap Brown prior to his conversion to Islam. That night, police officers pulled up to the Imam's convenience store with a warrant for his arrest. The police saw a man and asked him to put his hands up: 5'8", gray eyes, and 170 pounds, as eyewitnesses would later tell.

Asked to put his hands up, that man would instead pull out a handgun. A shootout between the man and two police officers would ensue. The man would then go to his trunk and pull out a lightweight, semi-automatic carbine Ruger Mini-14 with an extended clip housing 40 .223 caliber rounds of ammunition. Using military grade weapons, this man would murder one police officer and injure another. This man, Otis Jackson, would eventually confess to committing the crime.

Imam Jamil Al-Amin would be charged for this crime. Neither Jackson's confession of the crime nor his matching the description of the shooter would be included in Al-Amin's trial. For the jury, this evidence was nonexistent.

Eyewitness testimony claims that the man who killed the police officer was not only 5'8" and 170 pounds with gray eyes but also that he suffered gunshot wounds. While Jackson fits this description, Imam

Jamil Al-Amin is 6'5", lanky, has brown eyes, and did not suffer a single wound. A 911 call also claimed that the shooter was bleeding out and walking around West End looking for a ride.

Otis Jackson was on parole at the time of the shooting for a previous crime he had committed. He told his parole officer he had a shift working at a local diner at the time. When the officers told him to put his hands up, he felt the handgun in his pocket. Violating his parole and possessing an illegal weapon, Jackson knew that he would be sent back to jail. Aware of this, he decided to shoot at the police officers instead of putting his hands up.

That night, Jackson went home and received a call from Sentinel Company, which provided the monitoring for his ankle bracelet. The Sentinel representative asked where Jackson was, to which he replied he was at work. The representative then told Jackson that this would be marked down as a violation, to which Jackson agreed and quickly ended the conversation.

He then had female friends who were nurses come and treat him for his wounds. He told them that he was robbed. Jackson called a friend named Mustapha Tanner, and ask him to get rid of Jackson's vast arsenal of weapons: three Ruger Mini-14 rifles, an M16 assault rifle, a .45 handgun, three 9mm handguns and a couple of shotguns. He also informed his parole officer that he was involved in a "situation" but left out any details. Police later searched Jackson's house and found rounds of Mini-14, .223, 9mm, and M16 ammunition. His bloody clothes and boots from the shootout were left untouched in a closet.

His parole was revoked and he was sent to jail in Nevada. There he would confess to the crime and even be visited by an FBI agent by the name of Agent Devon Mahony. Jackson's confession was documented by Mahoney on June 29th, 2000. But nothing was done after that. Jackson's confession was also not included in Jamil Al-Amin's trial in March of 2002. In the midst of government surveillance on civil rights leaders and post 9/11 Islamophobia, Imam

Jamil Al-Amin would be sentenced to life without parole for the crime of murdering a police officer.

Al-Amin has an <u>appeal</u> on May 3rd in the 11th Circuit Court of Appeals that could potentially allow for a retrial. Through this retrial, it is possible that evidence that was previously left out of the court, such as Otis Jackson's testimony, could allow for Al-Amin to establish his innocence.

<u>Arrest and Trial</u>

Following this shooting, Imam Jamil Al-Amin would be put on the FBI's most wanted list, and 100 FBI agents would be deployed on a manhunt to find him. Al-Amin would be arrested in White Hall, Alabama four days later. As he was arrested, FBI agent, Ronald Campbell kicked and spit on him. It is important to note here that Imam Jamil Al-Amin was a 55-year-old religious leader. One would wonder what sort of hatred led an FBI agent to engage in such behavior towards a middle-aged clergyman.

Eventually, an officer would also find guns in the woods adjacent to where Al-Amin was found. Despite decades of FBI surveillance, there was absolutely no evidence linking Al-Amin to the guns. There was not a single fingerprint or Al-Amin's DNA on the guns or ammunition found. The guns were also not hidden or concealed in any way. *So under the state's argument, Al-Amin meticulously cleared the weapons of his DNA and fingerprints but did not do anything to hide the weapons.*

Many have suggested that it was actually Agent Campbell, the FBI agent who physically assaulted and spit on Imam Jamil Al-Amin, who planted the guns. In 1995, Campbell had been accused of shooting Glenn Thomas, an African American man, in the back of the head in Philadelphia. In that case, too, a fingerprint-less gun was found next to the man's dead body.

In addition, Agent Campbell first claimed that he was with other police officers when he crossed the fence into the woods and found the guns. But he later, under cross-examination, claimed that he was alone. Such contradictory information and the fact that the weapons could never be proved to belong to Al-Amin makes one wonder how this could function as any sort of evidence.

It is also important to note that Al-Amin went to trial in March of 2002, less than six months after 9/11. At a time when hatred against Muslims in the United States was at an all-time high, Al-Amin showed up to court wearing a kufi. He even said to the judge and jury: "I invite you to Islam. Be Muslim and receive two rewards [i.e. That of this life and the next]."

But even in this time when hatred of Muslims was at an all-time high, the idea of this soft-spoken Imam committing a crime was still strange to so many. The New York Times wrote that *"Some could not believe that the man who spent the last 25 years as a nonviolent Muslim cleric in the West End of Atlanta would explode in a seemingly unprovoked blaze of violence."*

Imam Jamil Al-Amin's Muslim faith was also attacked by the prosecution. They told the jury "Don't stand up for him," in reference to Al-Amin's religiously based decision to not stand for the court, for which the court granted him permission [not] to do.

The court ruled Al-Amin guilty and he was sentenced to life without parole. Following this the prosecuting attorney for the state said, **"After 24 years, we finally got him."** In order to understand the context of this remark, one must understand the COINTELPRO program that Al-Amin was targeted by before his conversion to Islam when he was H. Rap Brown.

Rap Brown & the Student Nonviolent Coordinating Committee

In his late teens, H. Rap Brown joined the Student Nonviolent Coordinating Committee. Known by its acronym, SNCC (*Pronounced "Snick"*) used the tactics of nonviolent direct action in order to bring about civil rights for Black Americans. Prominent in the American South, SNCC members studied Gandhian tactics of nonviolence from James Lawson, who was then a graduate student in theology at

Vanderbilt University. Future Congressman and then-SNCC Chairman, John Lewis would mentor H. Rap Brown.

In 1965, the young H. Rap Brown rose up in the organization and eventually became chairman of the Nonviolent Action Group, the Washington DC affiliate of SNCC. As head of this organization, Brown entered into an infamous White House meeting with President Lyndon B Johnson.

President Johnson told Brown that SNCC's all-night demonstration had prevented his two daughters from sleeping that night. Brown replied that he was sad for the one night his daughters were disturbed, but that *"Black people in the South had been unable to sleep in peace and security for a hundred years."* He asked what the President planned to do about that and anticipated that this issue was what this meeting was about.

Following John Lewis' tenure as chair of SNCC, Stokely Carmichael then became chair in 1966. Inspired by the works of Malcolm X and Frantz Fanon, Carmichael understood nonviolence not as a principle, but as a tactic. He introduced the phrase "Black Power' to the organization, and began to speak out on international issues, introducing SNCC's opposition to the American war in Vietnam.

FBI Surveillance on H. Rap Brown

In 1967, H. Rap Brown, at the age of 23, was elected Carmichael's successor as chairman of SNCC. Brown would take the nonviolent out of the name of the Student Nonviolent Coordinating Committee, renaming it the Student National Coordinating Committee. He lamented that, *"Violence is as American as cherry pie...We will use that violence to rid ourselves of oppression, if necessary. We will be free by any means necessary."* It was also under his leadership that SNCC entered into a working alliance with the Black Panther Party, giving Brown the honorary title of Minister of Justice of the Black Panther Party alongside being Chairman of SNCC.

That year, the FBI contacted Brown's wife, Karima Al-Amin, in an attempt to get her to spy on her husband for the FBI and provide reports on him to them. At this point, SNCC was being targeted by the FBI's COINTELPRO program, which aimed at surveilling, discrediting, and disrupting political organizations that fought for the rights of Black Americans. The FBI's COINTELPRO program called for H. Rap Brown and other prominent black leaders such as Martin Luther King Jr and Stokely Carmichael to be "neutralized."

It was through this program that J Edgar Hoover, head of the FBI, discovered that Martin Luther King Jr was having extramarital affairs. Attempting to use the tactic of public humiliation, Hoover wrote a letter to Martin Luther King Jr attempting to coerce him into suicide, lest he wants the world to know of his infidelity.

In December of 1969, two Black Panthers in Chicago fell victim to this neutralization after a 14-man police raiding force collaborated with the FBI. The police <u>murdered</u> 21-year-old, Fred Hampton and 22-year-old, Mark Clark, two members of the Black Panther Party in a pre-dawn raid in their Chicago home headquarters.

In a meeting with President Lyndon B Johnson, FBI Director Hoover said, in reference to Malcolm X and Martin Luther King Jr, "We wouldn't have any problem if we could get those two guys fighting; if we could get them to kill one another off."

This FBI campaign of neutralization caught up to H. Rap Brown. After giving a speech in Cambridge, Maryland, in July of 1970, he was grazed with bullets from police while walking a young woman home. That night fires occurred in the city. Brown would be accused of arson and inciting riots in the city. Later evidence would show Brown had nothing to do with the fires, and that they actually resulted from the inaction of the Cambridge Fire Department, which had a hostile relationship with its Black community. The head of the Cambridge Police Department pinned the charge on Brown, however, accusing him of "a well-planned Communist attempt to overthrow the government."

Congress would then pass the "H. Rap Brown law" in his name that would make it illegal to cross state lines in order to incite a riot. Then Governor of Maryland and soon-to-be Vice President of the United States, Spiro Agnew stated that "I hope they pick him up soon, put him away, and throw away the key."

Like many leaders in the movement such as Angela Davis, Brown would be placed on the FBI's Ten Most Wanted List and run away from the authorities, spending time in Africa before eventually being brought back to Maryland in 1970 for trial. It was there that he would be sentenced to 5 years at Attica Prison in New York City. In his time in prison, H. Rap Brown accepted Islam and took the name, "Jamil Abdullah Al-Amin."

Conversion to Islam and Reinvention as Jamil Al-Amin

Following his release from prison in 1976, Al-Amin traveled to India, Pakistan, and West Africa to study Islam. He then embarked upon travel to Makkah for the Hajj pilgrimage before moving to Atlanta to establish a Muslim community in the impoverished and crime-ridden West End neighborhood.

In the West End, the former radical firebrand reemerged as a pious, soft-spoken and bookish Muslim scholar, concerned about the spiritual and social resurrection of the neighborhood. He preached

Islam to drug dealers and prostitutes in the neighborhood and sought an intense anti-drug campaign.

In the West End Mosque, they called the adhan, the Muslim call to prayer, out loud five times a day, so that the whole neighborhood could hear it. Al-Amin was of the belief that change of society could only come after people had changed themselves through the act of prayer.

Imam Khalil Abdur-Rashid, the current Muslim Chaplain at Harvard University who grew up in Imam Jamil's West End community, mentioned in his Ph.D. dissertation:

He would retain his devotion to changing the prevailing system and worked to teach his community to cultivate an alternative way of living that is not indicative of token social justice programs. He taught the importance of the five pillars of Islam and revolutionary 'technologies of the self' that, when actualized at the communal level, transform the society into a better one. He still remained non-violent but still dedicated himself to teaching social revolution through a revolutionary approach to Islamic practice.

The mission of a believer in Islam is totally different from coexisting or being a part of the system. The prevailing morals are wrong. Western philosophy…has reduced man to food, clothing, shelter, and the sex drive, which means he doesn't have a spirit. In Islam, we're not talking about getting the poor to vote. We're not talking about empowering poor people with money. We're talking about overturning that whole thing.

He preached and wrote about the understanding of the centrality of prayer, charity, diet, pilgrimage, family, and struggle as the core elements of person and by extension social change. His book entitled, <u>Revolution By The Book</u>, published in 1994, is the first American Muslim liberation theology manifesto. Whereas much Christian liberation theology centralizes its attention on social concern for the poor and liberation of the oppressed, Imam Jamil's <u>Revolution By The Book</u> begins with the individual turning inward to correct decadent ways and through reform of the self, one may then begin to look outward at institutions that are also in need of reform. He explains that,

When you understand your obligations to God then you can understand your obligations to society. Revolution comes when human beings set out to correct decadent institutions. We must understand how this society has fallen away from righteousness and begin to develop, Islamically, the alternative institutions to those that are in a state of decline around us. But we must first enjoin right and forbid wrong within ourselves. That is the first step in turning this thing around: turn yourself around!

Many who had known him pre-conversion to Islam spoke of how much Al Amin had changed from the H. Rap Brown that once was. A former SNCC colleague, Ekwueme Michael Thelwell, commented on Al Amin's speech at the funeral of former SNCC Chairman, Stokely Carmichael. The talk included numerous other pillars of the civil rights movement such as John Lewis and Diane Nash. Thelwell <u>stated</u>:

The only real departure and my only surprise came when Imam Al-Amin spoke. What he delivered in tribute to his old friend was a thoughtful, Islam-inflected reflection on the nature of oppression and the moral duty, the religious imperative, of the faithful to resist. Liberally adorned with Koranic quotations, it was, as I recall, an erudite, elegantly constructed, finely reasoned explication of the categories and nature of oppression, and the moral dimensions and complexities of struggle as expressed in the prophetic poetry of the Arabian desert some 1,400 years earlier. In any terms–culturally speaking–it was scholarly. I found it startling in a curious way: It did not quite fit either stylistically or culturally with what had gone before yet was completely appropriate.

As he spoke, I remember thinking: Ah, so this is what a serious Islamic sermon sounds like, huh? Rap really takes this calling seriously. The brother is indeed an Islamic scholar, an imam. (I took in the hang-jawed look of astonishment and dawning professional respect that crossed Minister [Louis] Farrakhan's face as he listened, to be confirmation of my impression.

In an article titled *"Growing Up West End,"* Masood Abdul Haqq wrote about being a member of Imam Jamil Al Amin's West End community.

When my family and I first moved to Atlanta in the fall of 1992, the West End Muslim scene unfolded like some sort of Black Muslim Utopia. A soulful adhan was the soundtrack to Black children of all ages in kufis and khimars playing with each other on either side of the street. The intersecting streets near the masjid gave way to a large covered basketball court, on which the game in progress had come to a halt due to the number of players who chose to answer the melodic call to prayer. Overlooking this scene from the bench in front of his convenience store, like a shepherd admiring his flock, was a denim overall and crocheted kufi-clad Imam Jamil. *Before I heard him utter a single word, it was obvious to me that I was in the presence of a transcendent leader...*

FBI Perception of Al Amin Post-Conversion to Islam

Despite such transformation of self that led to the transformation of the West End community, Al-Amin still remained the object of government spying that went back to the COINTELPRO days. The FBI compiled a 44,000-word <u>file</u> on Al-Amin and his Muslim community, attempting to pin a crime upon him. Because his entire life was dedicated to praying five times a day at the mosque, developing his community, and stopping drugs and crime, the FBI could not find a single crime that Al Amin had committed.

After the 1993 bombing of the World Trade Center, Al Amin was <u>interrogated</u> by the FBI as to whether he played a role.

Al Amin's brother, Ed Brown <u>stated</u> that: *"Y'know...something happens. Say the first attempt to bomb the Trade Center, right? They feed their infallible profile into their computer. Muslim...radical...violent...anti-American, whatever, who knows. Anyway, boom, out spits the names, H. Rap Brown prominent among*

Two years following that, Al-Amin would be arrested by a joint taskforce of the FBI, local police, and the Bureau of Alcohol, Tobacco, Firearms, and Explosives after a 22-year-old, William Miles, was shot in the leg. One must wonder why the FBI was concerned about a non-fatal shooting that hit a young [black] man's right leg. But even in this case, Imam Jamil Al-Amin was found not guilty and cleared of any wrongdoing.

It was found that between 1992 and 1997, authorities investigated Al-Amin "in connection with everything from domestic terrorism to gunrunning to 14 homicides in Atlanta's West End." [Editor's note: A close Muslim confidant of Imam Jamil – Imam Luqman Ameen Abdullah - would also come under suspicion and surveillance, and be killed by police under questionable circumstances on October 28, 2009.]

While driving in Marietta, Georgia in May of 1999, Al-Amin would be pulled over in his vehicle for driving with a drive-out tag, which allows a vehicle to be driven without a license plate for 30 days. Eventually, Al-Amin would be searched, and an honorary police badge, given to him by the mayor of White Hall, Alabama, would be found in his wallet. Al-Amin was charged with impersonating a police officer, driving a stolen car, and driving with expired insurance. In 2002, a Georgia judge would rule that this warrantless search violated Imam Jamil Al-Amin's fourth amendment rights. The mayor of White Hall also wrote of how he had gifted Al-Amin this badge. Due to a snowstorm, Al-Amin's court date for this case was canceled— and never rescheduled.

It was this traffic stop that would lead to the arrest warrant. It was from that warrant that police officers would eventually be shot and killed by Otis Jackson, who would confess to the crime and match the description of the shooter. Despite this, it would be Imam Jamil Al-Amin who would go to jail.

Al-Amin's Time in Prison

In addition to being there for a crime that he claims he did not commit, Al-Amin has faced many violations of his rights in jail. He was unable to attend Friday prayers for years and has spent the bulk of his time in solitary confinement for 23 hours a day. Between June and August of 2003, the federal government was also caught reading his [legal] mail, in violation of Al-Amin's fourth amendment rights.

Despite his solitary confinement, word got around that Imam Jamil was imprisoned. Prisoners in Georgia also asked for Al-Amin to be their unified Imam "because of his credibility as a leader prior to incarceration," in an act that was not initiated by him. This led to an FBI investigation and report titled *"The Attempt to Radicalize the Georgia Department of Corrections Inmate Population,"* which established Al-Amin as the leader or this radical Muslim kingpin operating in prisons. The report failed to link Al-Amin to any extremist Muslim organization and also failed to establish how Al-Amin could lead such an extremist cell while being in solitary confinement.

Without notifying his family or legal counsel, Al-Amin was forcibly transferred by federal authorities in July of 2007. He was chained inside a vehicle for 6 hours in the 92-degree heat, while being deprived of his blood pressure medicine. Because he was unable to stand, Al-Amin was hospitalized for a night, before being transferred to the ADX prison facility in Florence, Colorado. He was then transferred to the United States Penitentiary in Arizona, a high-security federal prison for male inmates. In August of 2007, the Georgia Department of Corrections said Al-Amin was sent to federal prison because "Al-Amin's high profile presents unique issues beyond the state prison system's normal inmate." It was never explained what these "unique issues" are.

Appeal on May 3rd and Potential for Retrial

Allen Garrett is a lawyer who has been working pro-bono on Al-Amin's case since 2007. He <u>has</u> "discovered retaliatory actions on the part of prison officials against Al-Amin." Moreover, he has been granted the possibility for an appeal on May 3rd, in which the court will decide whether Al-Amin can be granted a retrial for the crime he was found guilty of in 2002.

With new evidence not included in the trial such as the confession of Otis Jackson, and Agent Campbell's lying about being alone and previous planting of fingerprint-less guns, Al-Amin has the potential to clear himself of such charges and establish his innocence. America too has changed drastically since Al-Amin was put on trial in 2002. Organizations such as Black Lives Matter have brought to light the injustice of programs such as COINTELPRO which targeted Al-Amin and other civil rights activists. The Trump era has also highlighted the irrationality of the brazen Islamophobia that aided Al-Amin's guilty verdict.

Al-Amin's membership in the Black Panther Party was symbolic and came as a result of an alliance between the Black Panther Party and the Student Nonviolent Coordinating Committee, which he was chair of. But despite his limited affiliation, in today's context, the Black Panthers do not have the same stigma attached to them. The movie, *Black Panther,* ends in Oakland, California, in an allusion to where the Black Panther Party was founded. Beyonce wore Black Panther outfits at the Super Bowl; and even Democratic Presidential candidate, Kamala Harris, hardly a symbol of radicalism or even progressivism, has stated that she was inspired by the values of the party.

I spoke to Kairi Al-Amin, Imam Jamil Al-Amin's son. He was 12 years-old when his dad was imprisoned. Since then, Kairi, now 31, has become an attorney, with the goal of freeing his dad of this crime that he did not commit. He spoke of the importance of getting public opinion on the side of his father as this appeal approaches. Should the court rule in favor of this appeal, a retrial could allow for evidence previously left out to be introduced. He has created a website called https://whathappened2rap.com/, which has a fact sheet on the trial, with information on how people can be better involved.

With the public watching, it is possible that on May 3rd the 11th Circuit Court of Appeals will rule in favor of Imam Jamil Al-Amin's retrial, and he can finally be given the opportunity to present the full case and be exonerated of this crime. [Editor's Note: The 11th Circuit Court of Appeals denied Imam Jamil's petition for a new trial, despite strong legal arguments in his favor, and the strong show of community support from around the US.]

Masood Abdul-Haqq: "Growing Up West End"

Masood Abdul-Haqq is a lover and writer of nonfiction. While managing a pediatrics clinic and juggling coursework in legal studies, Masood also teaches Qur'an class and serves as a board member at his local masjid. Masood resides in Oklahoma City with his wife and three children.

At the heart of the West End neighborhood of Atlanta is the Community Mosque, a quaint house, turned spiritual refuge, for Black Muslims from all over the country. In the early 1990s, at the heart of the Community Mosque, was Imam Jamil Al-Amin, a gangly, soft spoken man from Louisiana with a scruffy reddish brown beard and a knack for catchphrases that blended the latest hip hop slang into reminders about making 5 prayers a day. So when you heard him say he's checking you "because I'm Muslim by nature, not 'cause I hate ya," it made you realize that to be Black and Muslim was not only acceptable, it was downright cool. My introduction to Imam Jamil was not a direct one.

When my family and I first moved to Atlanta in the fall of 1992, the West End Muslim scene unfolded like some sort of Black Muslim Utopia. A soulful adhan was the soundtrack to Black children of all ages in kufis and khimars playing with each other on either side of the street. The intersecting streets near the masjid gave way to a large covered basketball court, on which the game in progress had come to a halt due to the number of players who chose to answer the melodic call to prayer. Overlooking this scene from the bench in front of his convenience store, like a shepherd admiring his flock, was a denim overall and crocheted kufi-clad Imam Jamil. Before I heard him utter a single word, it was obvious to me that I was in the presence of a transcendent leader.

The early 1990's was an exciting time to be in Atlanta. However, one of the unfortunate undercurrents of our booming urban economy was the inevitable rise of the drug trade. Reagan had been out of office for a full term, but his crack epidemic and trickle down economics were still very prevalent in inner city neighborhoods across the country. The West End was no exception. At the intersection of Holderness Street and Lucille Avenue, just 100 yards from my childhood home and four city blocks from the West End Masjid, stood a notorious motorcycle club and corner store. Both businesses were knee deep in the interests of prominent local drug dealers and it wasn't long before that corner earned the reputation as a "million dollar block."

One might think living so close to such a dangerous corner would make for a tale of hard knocks, peer pressure and intimidation. For the Muslim kids, that was the furthest thing from our reality. Instead, we ran around that neighborhood with impunity. When the dope boys saw us coming, they would step out of our way, offer to buy us snacks from the store, or just whisper to each other about us being "Big Slim's folks." Sometimes they called him Rap. Or the Imam. The bottom line was, they may have pulled the usual dope boy tricks of recruiting and terrorizing kids within the neighborhood, but us Muslim kids were off limits.

There was an honor associated with being a member of Imam Jamil's community, a VIP hood pass that made us immune to the usual ills of this sort of environment. This street credibility from outside the Muslim community stemmed from Imam Jamil's days as H. Rap Brown, a revolutionary fighting for Black rights. It evolved when he demonstrated the ability to bridge gaps between young and old, Muslim and non-Muslim. People respected that his entire life revolved around salat at the Masjid. This made him accessible and dependable.

Five times a day, the adhan was called and Imam Jamil would either lead or appoint someone to lead the prayer. Afterwards, no one would leave unless he raised his hand for permission and got the nod from the Imam. After finishing his dhikr and du'a, the Imam would ask, "Is there anything anyone would like to bring out?" Brothers would bring forth questions, concerns and news from around the neighborhood, and the Imam would address it or tell the person to meet him after salat. The drug issue was at the forefront. Slowly but surely, prayer by prayer, the million dollar block was abandoned. Miraculously, after efforts to clean up the neighborhood around the million dollar block, now stands the West End Islamic Center, a beacon of hope for sustaining the community.

One day after Asr salat, Imam Jamil asked, "is there anything anyone would like to bring out?" and my hand went up. All eyes turned to this 12 year old kid and I blurted, "Why do you always recite two surahs in every rakat? When you were out of town, the other brothers did the same thing. Is that some kind of Sunnah that I don't know?" I saw eyebrows going up and heads shaking all around the room. I felt like I made a huge mistake, but my curiosity had gotten the best of me. Imam Jamil smiled and replied, "I recite the surahs that have the most meaning, the most barakaat."

Later, he called me to the bench outside of his store to further explain his logic, dazzling me with his smooth way with words and sense of humor. For all of the intrigue, awe and fear that he inspires, the fact that Jamil Al-Amin was willing to take time to address me when he certainly had more pressing issues on his plate is what I remember most fondly about him. For all of his international acclaim and notoriety, he will always be the man that paved the way for me to grow up proud to be Black and Muslim.

Ambassador Andrew Young Calls for "Justice and Mercy"

An interesting opinion piece by Bill Torpy was published in the Atlanta-Journal Constitution newspaper on January 15, 2020. The title of the article, *"Why Andy Young seeks mercy for convicted killer Jamil Al-Amin."* What's striking is, much to the chagrin of the establishment, the former US ambassador to the United Nations (and Atlanta mayor) not only called for mercy, he raised questions about justice as well.

This respected elder and veteran of America's Civil Rights Movement was not the first to do so. Another prominent African American veteran of the movement raised her voice for fairness and justice when the trial was still underway.

Mrs. Coretta Scott King, the late widow of the Rev. Dr. Martin Luther King, Jr., wrote an open letter that was presented to me (to distribute as I saw fit) in the opening days of the 2002 trial. The most salient paragraph in her statement read: "For justice to be faithfully served, there must be no rush to judgment and the defense must be allowed to present all of its evidence, just as the prosecution must uphold the highest standards in meeting the burden of proof."

Mrs. King, founding president and CEO of *The King Center for Nonviolent Social Change,* ended up being strongly criticized in a number of editorials throughout the state…for simply calling for a fair proceeding!

In his article, Torpy described Andrew Young as "a national treasure located here in our backyard" – as he then proceeded to describe the occasion for which Ambassador Young was speaking. It was an event at Tyler Perry's studio "to commemorate the Fulton County district attorney's new Conviction Integrity Unit. The goal of the unit is to help free the wrongfully convicted or help shorten inordinately long prison sentences."

At one point, Young reportedly spoke about *"a case that weighs heavy on my heart because I really think he was wrongfully convicted."* The man, a Muslim, had helped "clean up" Atlanta's West End. *"I'm talking about Jamil Al-Amin,"* he said, *"H. Rap Brown."*

The wording here is very important. Ambassador Andrew Young is no stranger to this case, he has known Imam Jamil for decades and served as a character witness during the trial.

He further stated, according to the report, "I think it's time to re-judge. He's been dying of cancer and has been suffering away from his family in the worst prisons of this nation." Ambassador Young then reportedly turned to those in the new unit and said, "Anything you can do, even bring him home to be close to his family and friends," before concluding with, "We must stand for justice, but we must never forget mercy."

More often than not writers of articles of this nature for mainstream publications will exaggerate the state's evidence against the convicted prisoner and minimize evidence in the prisoner's favor. In political cases where the defendant has a history of resistance against the state, they will even introduce past alleged 'offenses' as circumstantial evidence as well. In the case of *'Jamil Abdullah Al-Amin verses the State of Georgia'* this is precisely what has consistently been done, throughout the US, from the beginning of this drama until now; while a truly objective review of this case reveals the fact that *exculpatory evidence* pointing to Imam Jamil's innocence has always been more weighty than the *inculpatory evidence* pointing to his guilt.

Imam Jamil's son, Attorney Kairi Al-Amin, has assumed a prominent role in the advocacy campaign around his father. He has disclosed the unfortunate fact that his father is now blind, the result of not receiving treatment for a serious eye condition, and that he is still fighting cancer in a federal prison hospital in Tucson, Arizona. The court battles have been so frustrating that he's concluded, "We will have to take this to the court of public appeal."

Let us hope, now that Ambassador Andrew Young has come out with such a strong statement of concern regarding the legitimacy of Imam Jamil's conviction and imprisonment, others who have remained shamefully silent will be able to find their voice and do the same…before it's too late!

Imam Khalid Griggs: Reflections on Imam Jamil Abdullah Al-Amin

Imam Khalid Abdul Fattah Griggs is the founding Imam of the Community Mosque of Winston-Salem (NC). He serves as Vice President of Social Justice and Civic Engagement of Islamic Circle of North America (ICNA), and editor of the organization's publication Message International Magazine. Imam Khalid is on the Board of the North Carolina-based Institute for Dismantling Racism. He is a freelance writer and human rights and prison reform activist

The second half of the 20th century produced arguably some of the most dynamic charismatic leaders from African nations and Black American communities in more than 100 years. Ahmed Sekou Toure of Guinea, Kwame Nkrumah of Ghana, Nelson Mandela of South Africa, and Patrice Lumumba of the Congo were just a few of the visionary leaders who lead liberation struggles against European colonial rule in their respective African countries.

Black America has given rise to Malcolm X (El-Hajj Malik El-Shabazz), Martin Luther King, Jr., Huey P. Newton, and, more recently, Rev. Dr. William Barber, III. These products from American soil consistently dedicated their adult lives to the struggle for human rights and dignity for all oppressed people generally and Black people in particular. To this latter group belongs Imam Jamil Abdullah Al-Amin, formerly H. Rap Brown.

From his days as H. Rap Brown to the present, Imam Jamil has been a fearless advocate for the victims of racist terrorist attacks and those denied rights as human beings and American and global citizens. Along with Malcolm X, Stokely Carmichael, and Robert Williams, H. Rap Brown was one of my childhood heroes. I first met the Imam in 1977 in his community store in Southwest Atlanta.

His weekly conversations with me were reserved for months as I checked in with him each week before returning to my work assignment as a union organizer in Southern Alabama; that is before I met Thomas Gilmore of Eutaw, Alabama. Gilmore was the first Black elected Sheriff in Green County Alabama. Known as the Sheriff without a gun, Gilmore had befriended and worked with Rap Brown when Brown was community organizing and doing voter registration for SNCC in the five counties known as the Black Belt.

Sheriff Gilmore asked me did I know his friend after learning that I was living in the Atlanta area. Gilmore called him "the most courageous man that I have ever known," who defined for him "manhood and showed me how to be a man." After sharing some of my conversations with Sheriff Gilmore to Imam Jamil, the Imam began to interact with me with a more relaxed demeanor.

H. Rap Brown inspired a generation of young people, after the assassination of Malcolm X, to take principled stands for justice. He is, to my knowledge, perhaps one of a few, if any, United States citizens to have inspired Congressional legislation to be commonly named after him. *The Rap Brown Law*, formally known as the "Civil Disobedience Act of 1968," was ostensibly enacted after his speech in Cambridge Maryland in 1967. Law enforcement officials asserted that he had crossed state lines to incite a civil disturbance that resulted that night in the firebombing of businesses and destruction of property.

Imam Jamil embraced Islam in 1971 and continues up to this moment to put his own life in danger to help other people. He is the embodiment of the hadith (sayings of Prophet Muhammad peace be upon him) to, "Let not fear of other people prevent one of you from speaking the truth, if he knows it."

Imam Jamil is a transcendent, inspirational, generational type of leader who appears only so often. I was enthralled by Imam Jamil when I visited him in Cobb County Jail after his arrest in 2000. Our visit ended with his signature departure statement of, "Do you need anything?" Such was the case with visits in Fulton County Jail and Canaan Federal Penitentiary in Waymart, Pennsylvania. We can ill afford to leave a life-long soldier for justice behind as if he is out of sight, out of mind.

May the Most High grant him healing as only He can, remove any cowardice from our hearts, and return Imam Jamil Abdullah Al-Amin to his family and us.

CHAPTER 6 - Where Do We Go from Here?

In this final action-oriented chapter we draw the readers' attention to the struggle ahead; and to some of things we can all do to help make a positive difference. Certain cases fall under the category of "litmus test" for the truly conscious folk in any society. The case of Imam Jamil Abdullah Al-Amin; Mumia Abu-Jamal; Leonard Peltier; and Dr. Aafia Siddiqui fall under the category of such cases, in my humble view. These cases represent a challenge to us all, and to the better of the "two Americas" – as defined by the late Senator J. William Fulbright. The chapter ends with thought-provoking final thoughts by the highly respected, Dr. Cornel West.

The US Supreme Court Affirms through its Denial

As we were putting the finishing touches on this manuscript a news report (dated April 6, 2020) quietly, but expansively, made it appearance in print and broadcast media nationwide – *"Supreme Court declines H. Rap Brown case."* The way the report read was virtually the same in all outlets. Here is the Associated Press release:

> WASHINGTON (AP) — The Supreme Court is declining to take the case of a 1960s black militant formerly known as H. Rap Brown who is in prison for killing a Georgia sheriff's deputy in 2000.
>
> As is usual, the justices didn't comment Monday in turning away Brown's case. Brown **had argued** his constitutional rights were violated at trial.
>
> Brown converted to Islam and now goes by the name Jamil Abdullah Al-Amin. He gained prominence more than 50 years ago as a Black Panthers leader and was at one point the chairman of the Student Nonviolent Coordinating Committee.
>
> In 2002, Al-Amin was convicted of murder in the death of Fulton County sheriff's Deputy Ricky Kinchen and the wounding of Kinchen's partner, Deputy Aldranon English. He was sentenced to life in prison.
>
> Al-Amin had argued that a prosecutor violated his right not to testify by directly questioning him during closing arguments in a sort of mock cross-examination.

The US Supreme Court's decision did not come as a surprise to me. Despite the clear judicial violations that took place throughout the trial; despite the exculpatory evidence kept out of the trial that pointed to his innocence; and despite the history surrounding this Muslim leader - and the national controversy which has surrounded this case from Day One – the highest court in the land decided that it should not be heard.

The court's decision is no more than an affirmation of the *Atlanta-Journal-Constitution's* 2002 editorial ("Al-Amin will die in prison, obscure and long forgotten") – and a challenge to those who oppose it.

The struggle continues!

Open Letter to the BOP and State of Georgia from Concerned Academics

We are academics who have spent our careers researching the history of the civil rights movement, issues of racial discrimination in the United States, civil rights law, and the representation of minorities in the public sphere. We strongly believe that deepening knowledge of our nation's past is essential to informing progress in American politics and race relations today.

The acquisition of historical knowledge is strengthened considerably by having living participants in those histories recount their experiences. We are therefore dismayed to learn of the current restrictions placed upon one such prominent participant, Jamil Abdullah Al-Amin (formerly known as H. Rap Brown).

During the 1960s, Al-Amin was a national leader of the civil rights movement and was chair of the Student Non-Violent Coordinating Committee, one of the era's key organizations. As a civil rights leader, he met with President Johnson, spoke across the country, and appeared regularly in television interviews. He is currently an inmate at the federal prison at Tuscon, Arizona. He has been held in federal custody, on behalf of the Georgia Department of Corrections, since 2007.

Throughout the last decade, all requests for interviews by scholars and journalists have been denied by the Federal Bureau of Prisons. Their decision is, in part, based on the Georgia Department of Corrections' view that Al-Amin is ineligible for interviews "due to the potential security risks." Letters to and from Al-Amin are usually held by the government for months before they are released. In these ways, Al-Amin is prevented from any form of practical communication with scholars who wish to document this history.

We understand that Al-Amin has been convicted of an extremely serious charge. However, we do not believe there is any reasonable basis upon which to deny him direct access to scholars and journalists.

His story ought to be documented for posterity. In-person interviews with him in prison are essential for this purpose because he is seventy-four years old and is serving a life sentence without parole.

We thus declare our opposition to the restrictions placed upon Al-Amin and call on the Georgia Department of Corrections and Federal Bureau of Prisons to allow scholarly and media interviews and communication with Al-Amin. We will make the reasons for our consternation known to our own elected representatives and the public at large.

Special note: Over 100 academics from the US and abroad signed this petition, addressed to the U.S. Bureau of Prisons and the State of Georgia, requesting access to Imam Jamil Abdullah Al-Amin (the former H. Rap Brown). To see the full list of names go to:
https://www.kundnani.org/jamilalamin/

Imam Jamil Action Network (IJAN) Statement

IJAN's theme for the year 2019 is, *"From H. Rap Brown to Imam Jamil Al-Amin, Seventy-five Years of Life, Sixty Devoted to Conscious Struggle: A PRISONER AT WAR."*

For over fifty of those sixty years of conscious struggle there is documented evidence of the fabrication of legal cases against H. Rap Brown who later became known as Imam Jamil Abdullah Al-Amin. In mid-April of this year (2019) the 11th Circuit Court of Appeals announced its intention to hear oral arguments in the case of Jamil Abdullah Al-Amin. The date set for those oral arguments was May 3, 2019.

On July 31, 2019, judges of the 11th Circuit announced their regret for being "unable to offer Mr. Al-Amin any relief." The primary issue argued and denied was the violation of Imam Jamil's Constitutional rights. The court was to determine if illegal actions committed by the prosecution caused any harm to the defendant's right to a fair trial. The court ruled it didn't, even though an interview with a juror in the case (conducted before the 11th Circuit decision to hear oral arguments) revealed that the prosecutor's remarks were the deciding factor that persuaded the interviewed juror to vote guilty.

From the very beginning of this case Imam Jamil Al-Amin has proclaimed and maintained his innocence, and there is a preponderance of evidence to support his claim. In the interest of "justice" the question that many who have been following this case asked before and after the May 3rd hearings is: 'Why is it we only have hearings on (comparatively speaking) minor issues that have come about as a result of major gross miscarriages of justice?'

Among the gross miscarriages of justice which have plagued this case are the following:

- The judge in a Cobb County courtroom in January 2000, who closed the court and sent Imam Jamil Al-Amin home (due to adverse weather conditions); who a few hours later re-opened the court and issued an arrest summons for Jamil Al-Amin for "failure to appear."

- The tragic shooting incident in which one sheriff's deputy was killed and another seriously injured during an alleged attempt to serve a bogusly issued summons (the night before a major holiday in the Muslim calendar).
- The heightened hysteria and actual arrest of Imam Jamil, even after eye witness' descriptions of the assailant in that shooting did not even closely resemble the imam.
- The actions of a rogue FBI agent, Ron Campbell, who said (on the night of the arrest) if his unit had caught up with him first, 'Mr. Al-Amin would not be alive.'
- The prosecution hid from the defense team the fact that the State of Nevada had someone in custody who fit the description initially given of the assailant that night; someone who actually confessed to being the shooter of the sheriff's deputies (Otis Jackson).
- The meetings that took place in the presiding judge's chambers with FBI officials - that state prosecutors and defense attorneys were barred from.

IJAN invites justice-loving people to join our campaign and help expose the truth regarding the life and legacy of Imam Jamil Abdullah Al-Amin (formerly H. Rap Brown), and the U.S. government's decades long conspiracy against him.

Visit us on Facebook (Jamil Action Network). Also visit: www.whathappened2Rap.com

A Message from Kairi Al-Amin

As-Salaamu Alaikum,

As you may know, my father, Imam Jamil Al-Amin, formerly H. Rap Brown civil rights leader and humanitarian, was convicted of a murder he did not commit in 2002.

Upon that conviction, we essentially abandoned him. No tangible noise was ever made and as such, my father's conviction and subsequent exile, a vendetta realized, has gone unchecked. The cruel and unusual punishment; the confession of another man; the medical neglect in the hope that he dies; the gag order; the federal holding of a state prisoner away from his attorney's and family; we've done nothing about anything and because of our lack of action, much like the man himself, the truth about this case and his legacy have been erased from public view.

If we don't commit to action, the same action he dedicated himself to for the entirety of his life, the same action many of you are benefiting from while he sits suffering silently, then we have turned our backs on our Imam...your brother and we should be ashamed.

We have been fighting this fight in the courts for 20 years and because the outward appearance is that "his people don't even care about him," we haven't gotten anything more than, "yes he deserves a new trial but no you can't have one," and again that's on us because what have we done about it?

Alhamdulillah, we've been afforded yet another opportunity, and this time we aren't even asking you to decide his guilt or innocence, though it should be obvious. We are only asking that you help him get the opportunity to prove his innocence to you and salvage his name. A fair trial, where the man who confessed to this crime actually testifies, where constitutional rights are respected, and where the state prosecutors misconduct is not overlooked and subsequently rewarded with a federal judgeship. No, we want a fair trial...that's all.

That being said, if you can get behind the idea of Imam Jamil, or anyone for that matter, finally receiving a fair opportunity to prove their innocence, then please, sign and share our petition.

We must let District Attorney Paul Howard and The Fulton County Conviction Integrity Unit know that we are paying attention and we demand fairness and justice at the very least.

Meet me on the front line: https://www.change.org/freeimamjamil

Sincerely,

Kairi Al-Amin
Attorney & Son of Imam Jamil Al-Amin FKA H. Rap Brown
https://whathappened2rap.com/

Make The Fulton County Conviction Integrity Unit Do What It Says It Does!

Looking Back to Look Ahead

While wrongful imprisonment is an oppressive stain on any nation, and should be of concern to us all, I want to address these concluding remarks specifically to two distinct segments of the US population: African Americans and Muslims (of all tribes).

Some folk are uncomfortable with talking about or associating themselves with Imam Jamil's "H. Rap Brown" past, but a person's past is an indelible part of who he or she is. As Wordsworth once said, *"Child is the father of man."* To fully understand the man you must first examine his past. The past of Imam Jamil is one imbued with challenge, controversy, and noble struggle - despite any and all discomforting warts.

The objective of the establishment was made clear after the imam's conviction and sentencing in 2002 - *"Al-Amin will die in prison, obscure and long forgotten"* (Atlanta Journal Constitution, 3/13/02). The determination of America's freedom fighters, and the communities they represent, must be equally resolute. With that being said, I begin this challenging summation by addressing the members of Imam Jamil's tribe (in the "racial" context).

When this tragedy first erupted on March 16, 2000, the establishment's prosecutorial game plan was immediately apparent – both in the "court of public opinion" and later in a "court of law." It would use both race and religion to prosecute a man with a sterling history of defending both. They would use the fact that two black sheriff's deputies were the victims of an alleged Muslim perpetrator's rampage; they would use the alleged perpetrator's faith (Islam) as a weapon of prejudice against him.

This was easy to do for a couple of reasons. Fear and bias against Islam and Muslims had already been stoked throughout America for years; evidenced by an observation made by the late William 'Bill' Kunstler in his thought-provoking biography titled, <u>My Life As A Radical Lawyer</u>. In a chapter titled, "The Despised Muslim," he wrote the following words: "Today Muslims are the most hated group in

America. The moment a Muslim is accused of a crime the specter of terrorism is raised and everyone panics." The panic that Kunstler so ably described in 1994 was/is a cultivated reaction by skillful propagandists. A reaction aided by the fact that the playing field in this case was Georgia, part of America's "Bible Belt" in the "new south!"

The state chose a young, black, ambitious prosecutor by the name of Paul Howard to lead the charge against this long-vilified nemesis of the status quo. Regretfully, *most* of Atlanta's black establishment (including most of Metro-Atlanta's black Muslim establishment) either went along with the game plan or remained dutifully quiet. The State's nefarious agenda was also aided by two things – the tragedy of September 11th (just seven months later), and communal ignorance regarding this man and his rich legacy of struggle during one of the most turbulent and defining decades in American history.

Some years after his brutal banishment into the American gulag – a "supermax" / federal ADX prison in Florence, Colorado, where he remained in solitary confinement - Imam Jamil became gravely ill. This prompted an urgent response from family, friends, and supporters who had not forgotten him. An editorial was published in the May 27, 2014, edition of "The Final Call" newspaper. The caption read, *"A Black Liberation Soldier Needs Help!"* While the caption said all that needed to be said, for any African American acquainted with their history, the final paragraph in the editorial left no room for doubt as to what our response should be: "Imam Al-Amin has stood for you and me, and a letter or phone call showing support should not be too much for us to do. A man has lost his freedom and now sits suffering in prison. We are free to act, but will we?"

The response to that 2014 medical crisis was admirable nationwide - and included at least one African American congressman. It resulted in Imam Jamil being transferred to a penal medical center in Butner, NC, for emergency treatment; and further, not being sent back to the "supermax" prison in Colorado after the treatment ended. A little over five years later, the health of Imam Jamil – a man who many believe to be an innocent target of a never-ending government conspiracy - is once again in a critical state! And thus, that rhetorical question raised in "The Final Call" editorial still remains relevant.

To my Muslim brethren: If we truly understand our Islam we would realize the special obligation we have to Imam Jamil Abdullah Al-Amin; both because he is an oppressed human being, and because he is a Muslim with a sterling legacy of struggle that spans decades. I often refer to Imam Jamil as a bridge between two generations of political prisoners in America, a powerful symbol of the cyclical nature of never-ending struggle. The powers-that-be know this; and this is precisely why they keep him off limits to writers, researchers, historians, and the like! In the *"Other Voices"* chapter of this treatise the reader got a glimpse into just how transformative a figure this respected elder truly is, and the impact he's had on others.

Imam Jamil is no stranger to the Muslim community in America (immigrant or indigenous). Beyond the role he has played in helping to expand Muslim organizational presence in the US, I sometimes remind my immigrant brethren of the fact that there is no path to power or security in the United States (for any minority) that does not intersect with black roots. The life and legacy of H. Rap Brown/Imam Jamil Abdullah Al-Amin symbolizes this reality.

The last divinely sent Messenger of Allah (God Almighty) to all humanity, Mohammed ibn Abdullah (peace be upon him) is reported to have said: *"May Allah brighten the face of a man who hears me and then relays to another who has not. It is possible that a carrier of knowledge is himself not knowledgeable, or that the carrier of knowledge will deliver it to someone more knowledgeable. Three things purify the heart of a Muslim: the sincerity in working for the sake of Allah; taking up the task of advising the rulers; and not departing [separating oneself] from the body of Muslims."*

Sheikh Ibn Taymeeyah (a learned scholar and political prisoner of an earlier age) made the following observation concerning the aforementioned hadith (oral tradition) during a tumultuous period in his own life:

In order to implement this principle on a personal note, I say that it is not my wish for any Muslim to be harmed because of me overtly or covertly. This applies to all Muslims, but more specifically to our companions and acquaintances. Neither do I want any of them to be blamed or condemned, as they are still worthy of honor and respect. Indeed, man does not escape being classified into one of three categories: a correct mujtahid (seeker of knowledge), a wrong one, and a sinner. The first is rewarded and praised, the second is rewarded yet forgiven for his blunder. Regarding the third, I ask Allah to forgive him, us, and the rest of the Muslims.

Therefore, we shall turn a new leaf on those who had erred and not fulfilled this aforementioned principle. Yet I know of some who say, "This man erred." And "This man did not do what he should have [done]" or "The Shaykh was harmed because of this man." Those words that have harmed some brothers I do not condone, nor do I pardon those who utter them.

You should all know that we are joining to assist one another. It is obligatory upon us to aid each other, more so now than before. So, whosoever thinks that harming some brothers as a result of the hardship experienced in Damascus and Egypt is warranted, then he is wrong. It is true that a believer to a believer is like the two hands, one cleans the other. And it is also true that some kind of dirt can only be washed by hard scrubbing, yet this treatment will be justified when the outcome appears to be the restoration of that lost brotherly love.

Let no one think that the believers can be economical with helping their brothers, and in aiding them. If some of our companions had neglected us before, then came to us, their status will rise higher than before. You might also know – may Allah be pleased with you - that issues like this one often

*occur due to a difference of opinion and variations that might
even befall the people of iman (faith), due to the whispers of
shaytan (the accursed enemy of God and humanity).*

The Muslim Challenge

"The stronger Islam becomes in America the more government
will focus its attention on undermining it, distorting it, and employing
its counterintelligence tactics to discredit it, and finally outright
attacking it. It shows our utter ignorance to the nature and history of
this taghuti system when Muslims smile and boast about how
benevolent Uncle Sam is towards the Muslims in America, and how
much "freedom" Muslims have to practice Islam. There is the *illusion*
of freedom only when Muslims do not address the concrete issues that
impact the people; and when they avoid identifying the oppressor for
what and who he truly is; and when they support the laws, policies and
very guise for taghut (tyranny) to exist and govern." -Jihad Abdul
Mumit *("49 Points of Attention")*

When Abdul Mumit (a former political prisoner himself) wrote
these words in 1997 he was right on the mark. Muslims today, if their
eyes are open and their vision is clear, should be able to see the
significance of these words with even greater clarity. The plight of
Imam Jamil Abdullah Al-Amin should not be viewed in isolation; it is
part of a larger mosaic of oppression that views the deen of Islam as
Public Enemy Number One. For those inclined to casually dismiss
such observations as coming from angry "extremist Muslims," reflect
once again on the words of [former US Attorney General] Ramsey
Clark: "There can be no question that the United States government –
through its intelligence agencies and most of its appointed leadership,
and a great deal of its elected leadership – considers Islam, not just
militant Islam, but Islam, to be the greatest threat to the domestic and
international security of the United States."

This was the sober-minded reflection of a former high-ranking
government official, and internationally renowned human rights

advocate. Mr. Clark is well acquainted with US history and the "two Americas" - of which the late US Senator J. William Fulbright spoke so eloquently in his thought-provoking work titled <u>The Arrogance Of Power</u>.

Muslims are commanded in The Noble Qur'an to, "Stand firmly for justice as witnesses to ALLAH (God Almighty), even if it be against yourselves…." We are also commanded by our Prophet (peace be upon him) thusly, "When you see an evil action, you must change it with your hand; if you cannot do so, with your tongue; if you cannot do so, [detest it] within your heart – and know that this is the weakest degree of faith." ALLAH's Messenger also said, "One of the greatest jihads is to speak truth to a caliph [or other governing authority] who has deviated from the right way."

We have a responsibility to help our nation, wherever we may be, live up to the better part of itself. We cannot do this by being timid, or afraid, or complicit. One of the rightly guided successors of Prophet Mohammed (pbuh), a member of his noble family, Imam Ali ibn Abu-Talib (may ALLAH be pleased with him), is reported to have said: "Three classes of men [and women] are cut off from the blessings of Paradise: oppressors; those who aid oppression; and those who tolerate oppression."

Finally, against the backdrop of a global pandemic (Novel Coronavirus, aka COVID-19) we have a reminder from The Noble Qur'an: **"No calamity occurs except by the permission of ALLAH."** On a related note, we also have the words of two prominent personalities in world history – one from the eastern tradition, the other from the western tradition – from two different eras saying essentially the same thing.

Sheikh ibn Taymeeyah: "Civilization is based on justice, and the consequences of oppression are devastating. Therefore, it is said ALLAH aids the just state, even if it is non-Muslim; and withholds His help from the oppressive state, even if it is Muslim."

Thomas Jefferson: "I tremble for my country when I reflect, God is just; His justice cannot sleep forever."

Oppression, in all of its many forms, has settled upon almost every part of ALLAH's earth; the tribulation of our time may be viewed as a punishing wake-up call and a warning. The question for us today is: Who will heed the warning?

In the struggle for peace thru justice,

El-Hajj Mauri' Saalakhan

Dr. Cornel West: Final Thoughts

"Let Not Fear of Other People
Prevent One of You from Speaking the Truth,
If He Knows It"

The Black freedom struggle is the greatest tradition of spiritual fortitude and moral courage in the modern world. In the face of White supremacist hatred, capitalist greed and American terror – for over 400 years – we have unleashed magnificent love warriors and lionhearted fighters for Black honor and human self-determination. Imam Jamil Abdullah Al-Amin (formerly known as H. Rap Brown) belongs within the pantheon of the cloud of witnesses who sacrificed life and limb to keep alive the Black Freedom Struggle.

Born in Louisiana, educated at Southern University and Howard University as well as nurtured in the streets and roads of Mississippi, Imam Jamil Abdullah Al-Amin emerged as a bold son of Malcolm X – namely a genuine lover of Black people and a fearless spokesman for Black self-respect, self-defense and self-determination. The Black Freedom struggle has always been an anti-terrorist movement – a spiritual and physical war against niggerization and repression. Niggerization keeps Black people scared, intimidated and fearful of White supremacist power. Repression keeps Black people incarcerated and imprisoned – or assassinated and subordinated. The fundamental aim of a great freedom fighter like Imam Jamil Abdullah

Al-Amin has been to de-niggerize himself and others and preserve his dignity and grace in the face of massive and perpetual U.S. state repression. His classic autobiography Die Nigger Die (1969) is a two-fold cry of the heart to both extricate the fear and enact the love that embraces death for the cause of Black honor and liberty.

Like Martin Luther King Jr.'s favorite saying, "I would rather be dead than afraid," Imam Jamil Abdullah Al-Amin put his life and body on the line over and over again. Again like Martin Luther King, Jr., who emerged from the paddy wagon on his way to Reidsville State Prison in Tattnall County, Georgia, from a four-hour ride in the pitch-black with a German shepherd threatening him saying, "This is the Cross that we must bear for the freedom of our people!" Imam Jamil Abdullah Al-Amin (who also was incarcerated in that same prison) has paid an indescribable price for bearing a Cross of service to a hated, haunted and hunted Black people. Like Malcolm X, Imam Jamil Abdullah Al-Amin is a revolutionary Muslim and a pioneer in Islamic Liberation Theology with his powerful book, <u>Revolution by the Book</u> (the Rap is Live) (1993). His student and my dear brother, Chaplain Khalil Abdur Rashid of Harvard University, represents the best of this prophetic Islam.

The cruel and atrocious treatment of Imam Jamil Abdullah Al-Amin – from the H. Rap Brown law passed by Congress to target him and other Freedom Fighters, the Cointelpro attacks on him and others to the tortuous solitary confinements in U.S. barbaric prisons – has not squelched his soul nor suffocated his spirit. He remains a de-niggerized, dignified Free Black man grounded (with great scholarly and ritual fervor) in his deep Muslim faith, and forever a Titan in any history of the Black Freedom Struggle. Let us never forget his loving sacrifice and steadfast service to us!

What YOU Can Do

Connect with the Imam Jamil Action Network (IJAN):

Midwest Region: (216) 215-0165
Northeast: (215) 738-8807
South: (252) 907-4443
West Coast: (510) 282-2587

Support 'The Awareness Campaign' and Documentary (in the making) via: whathappened2rap.com – led by Kairi Al-Amin.

To write Imam Jamil:
Jamil A. Al-Amin
99974-555
USP Tucson
U.S. Penitentiary
P.O. Box 24550
Tucson, AZ. 85734

Please be advised that due to a serious vision impairment that he has not been receiving treatment for, it may not be possible for Imam Jamil to respond to your correspondence in a timely manner. Another way to support the "Awareness Campaign," and The Aafia Foundation's work for Imam Jamil (and others), is by sharing this publication with as many folk as you possibly can. **Information Is Power**, and good books make great gifts!

About the Author

El-Hajj Mauri' Saalakhan is a Metropolitan Washington, DC-based human rights advocate, writer, lecturer and poet. His work has taken him across America into Africa, Europe, the Indian subcontinent, and the Middle East.

In 1999, he served as a consultant for Amnesty International's year-long focus on human rights abuses in the United States.

Saalakhan is the author of several human rights-oriented publications on issues at home and abroad. As a critically acclaimed poet and community activist, he was selected as *"An Outstanding Young Man of America"* in 1986. In 1995 he was the recipient of the *"Dr. Martin Luther King, Jr. Award"* from the Southern Christian Leadership Conference (SCLC), a *"Maryland State Senate Resolution,"* and a *U.S. Congressional Letter of Commendation* - for his human rights work throughout Metropolitan Washington, DC.

He co-founded the Coalition Against Political Imprisonment and the National Association for Police Accountability. He is a founding member of the Coalition for Civil Freedoms (aka, National Coalition to Protect Civil Freedoms); and founding Director of The Peace *Thru* Justice Foundation. He currently serves as Director of Operations for The Aafia Foundation, Inc. – a Muslim-led human rights organization based in Maryland (aafia.org).

El-Hajj Mauri' Saalakhan is available for speaking engagements on a variety of social, political, and human rights issues. He can be reached via: **E-mail:** peacethrujustice@aol.com / **Twitter:** @maurisaalakhan **Mobile:** (202) 246-9608.

www.ingramcontent.com/pod-product-compliance
Lightning Source LLC
Chambersburg PA
CBHW070702250726

48662CB00001B/225